FINLAND

by J. Hampden Jackson

ENGLAND SINCE THE INDUSTRIAL REVOLUTION
EUROPE SINCE THE WAR
POST-WAR WORLD

edited by J. Hampden Jackson

MODERN HISTORY OF EUROPE
OUTLINE OF EUROPEAN HISTORY

FINLAND

by

J. HAMPDEN JACKSON

NEW YORK
THE MACMILLAN COMPANY
1940

Reprinted February, 1940

Reprinted March, 1940

PRINTED IN THE UNITED STATES OF AMERICA

Acknowledgement

To Mr. Paavo Soukka, who watched over the manuscript of this book with a guardian's eye, and to Dr. Jussi Teljo, who read it with an historian's, the particular thanks of the author are due.

Contents

Maps and Diagrams

CHAPTER I

INTRODUCTION

"The history of all these Northern countries well deserves far more attention from Englishmen than it has hitherto received."

LORD BRYCE

No one can be surprised that English-speaking people take so little interest in Finland. It is the fault of the atlases and the history text-books. The maps show Finland as a semi-arctic country lying between the same unattractive latitudes as Greenland; they fail to show that her northernmost coast is ice-free all the year round and that the whole country enjoys a summer that is hotter, if a trifle shorter, than that of the British Isles. The histories treat Finland as an insignificant province first of Sweden, then of Russia; they show her as a satellite in the meteoric career of the Vasas or as an outlandish star in the constellation of the Great Russian Bear. In this telescopic treatment Finland never quite comes into focus. Of the ten thousand pages of the *Cambridge Modern History* not two consecutive pages are devoted to Finnish affairs between the fifteenth century and the twentieth. And of the period of her independent nationhood academic historians have nothing to say: they prefer to leave the study of the contemporary to writers who can afford to make mistakes. Altogether they fail to impress upon us that the Finns have developed their culture and institutions through long centuries of invasion and conquest, and have emerged in our own time as an independent republic owing nothing to the fortuitous boundary-drawing of the drafters

13

of the Treaty of Versailles. Nor do bolder writers suggest that there is anything of moment to be learned from the country which so many of them vacantly describe as the Land of Ten Thousand Lakes.

There is nothing surprising about this lack of interest, but it is none the less regrettable. One might have thought that sentimental reasons would have been enough to arouse interest in Finland. After all it was an Englishman who first brought Christianity to that country, another Englishman who built her first cathedral, and another Englishman—or rather a Scotsman—who built her first cotton-mill. Scotsmen have found a home in Finland since the seventeenth century; apparently they have also found a career, for there are Ramsays, Keiths, Frasers, Hamiltons, and Douglases there to-day. Gratitude, one might have thought, would have compelled English-speaking people to some study of the country whence came the tar which held together her wooden bulwarks, the masters under whom so many of her seamen served their apprenticeship in sail, and the lumbermen who proved most efficient in clearing the virgin forests of North America. And if gratitude is a doubtful tie, self-interest is a strong one. The United States can ill afford to ignore a race to which nearly three hundred thousand of her citizens belong. Great Britain can ill afford to remain in ignorance of a people who spend more (per person) on British goods than any other nation in the world except Denmark and Norway.

There are weightier reasons for calling attention to Finland. In these days when the increasingly popular view is that Europe is faced by an alternative between Communism or some form of Fascism it is particularly important to stress the possibility of a middle way. In these days when faith in the liberal creed and in democratic institutions is waning, it is more important than ever before to study the countries where that creed and those institutions are still in the ascendant. They are in the ascendant particularly in the northern countries. Norway, Sweden, Denmark and Finland have found a middle way between private enterprise and State control. In each of these countries, where the Social Democrats form the largest single party, capitalism in peasant dress has triumphed, capitalism shorn of its nineteenth-century ruthlessness and trimmed to the equalitarian ideals of the twentieth. In each there is a more real equality of opportunity than in England; in each the distance between the rich and the poor is shorter. The middle way has been easy for Norway where industrialism on a large scale has never been a temptation; it has not been difficult for Sweden with her long individualist tradition; even for Denmark it will not be difficult so long as she remains assured of the economic patronage of Great Britain. But for Finland it has been an uphill fight. She was still part of the Russian Empire when the great war broke out; since the war she has undergone a Communist insurrection and a Fascist *putsch*, yet to-day Finland is an independent democratic republic. Her people owe much to Germany, but they have no Nazi sympathies; their frontier marches with that of the Soviet Union, their capital is within an hour's flight of Leningrad, but in Finland Communist propaganda cuts no ice. Of all the neighbours of Soviet Russia there is none which enjoys such a high degree of political liberty. The best criticism of Soviet Communism is to be found in the attitude which has been maintained towards it across the Finnish frontier. The best demonstration of the vitality of parliamentary democracy and of its power to adapt itself under the greatest difficulties is to be found in Russia's north-western neighbour.

There is a second pressing political problem for which something approaching a solution has been found in Finland, namely, that of combining two distinct races in one united nation without allowing one to oppress the other. It is a problem which has had a peculiar fascination for English-speaking people. It baffled our statesmen in Canada, though solution there was comparatively easy thanks to the localization of the French community. It is still baffling them in South Africa, in Palestine, and in Ireland. The parallel between Ireland and Finland is singularly close. Eric of Sweden invaded Finland in almost the same year that Henry II was invading Ireland. In each case the conquest bred a new race in the conquered country: in one the Anglo-Irish, in the other the Swedo-Finn. In each the settler-people swamped the culture of the natives and set the pace of the new civilization. In each the natives preserved their language[1] and, within living memory, asserted their claim to economic equality and to political power. And there the parallel ends. The English conquerors were as misguided as the Swedish were wise; the Irish question still troubles England, but there has long

[1] Finnish belongs to what philologists call the Ugro-Finnish group of languages and has no resemblance to any other European tongue except Estonian and early Magyar. Hardly a word in the vocabulary would be recognized by any Swedish, German or Russian speaking person, and the grammar and syntax are extraordinarily complicated. There are no articles, no gender, no letters *b*, *c*, *f*, *q*, or *w*, and no prepositions—their place being taken by fifteen case-endings. By way of compensation, Finnish is relatively easy to pronounce. The stress is on the first syllable of each word and every written letter is articulated; long vowels and consonants are indicated by double letters, the Finnish *y* is roughly the German *ü* and the *ä* and *ö* are not unlike broader versions of the German modified vowels.

ceased to be a Finnish problem for Sweden. The Gaelic enthusiasts were as uncompromising as the Finns in their triumph were generous; the Gaels have not yet found a *modus vivendi* with the Anglo-Irish, while the Finns have reconciled, if they have not finally appeased, the Swedo-Finns. It is said that Arthur Griffith founded the Free State with an essay on Hungary; he might have founded it more securely with a study of the Finns (who, incidentally, are racially connected with the Magyars). The truth is that statesmen of London and Dublin—to say nothing of Belfast—have a lesson to learn from the history of Finland.

But an altogether larger problem is posed by the achievements of contemporary Finland in other spheres. That little country—its population is only 3,700,000, though in area it ranks seventh in Europe—has produced the greatest musician of our day. Sibelius is as pre-eminent among symphonic composers of the early twentieth century as Beethoven in the early nineteenth. He has lived his life in his native Finland and is conscious of the national sources of his inspiration. His music is intensely national, it is as Finnish as Beethoven's was German, though it would be as futile to look for Finnish mythology in the tone-poem he dedicated to the Forest God *Tapio* as to look for German history in the symphony which Beethoven dedicated to Napoleon. Sibelius is not the only musician of international renown which his country has produced; the names of Palmgren and Melartin, of Kuula and Kilpinen, are not unknown abroad, and in the Carelian province there is a popular musical tradition comparable with—though of course very different from—that of Wales. And music is not the only art in which the Finns have excelled. One of the greatest living exponents of the architectural art, as of the musical, is a native of Finland. Saarinen, before he crossed the Atlantic to give grace and strength to the megalomaniac buildings of Chicago, made Helsinki (Helsingfors)[1] one of the two or three first cities of the world for students of modern architecture. There remained several architects in Finland fit to rank with Saarinen, as Siren's Diet building and Alvar Aalto's Library at Viipuri (Viborg) will prove. Even better known than these achievements in the arts is Finland's pre-eminence in physical culture. Success in international competitions proverbially goes to the rich rather than to the strong, but Finland was second in the Olympic Games of 1912, of 1920, of 1924 and of 1928, second in 1932, second again in 1936. This is an astonishing record for a poor country which has never countenanced professionalism in sport and which only lately began to organize athletic training.

It cannot be an accident that this new nation has made such a disproportionate contribution to the aesthetic and physical culture of our times.

The question arising here is one that will never cease to puzzle historians: what is the relation, if any exists, between the geographic, economic and social conditions of a country and its achievements in the arts and sciences?

The geographer would have his answer pat. Finland, he would say, is a vast granite plain broken by sixty thousand lakes: what more natural than that it should breed a race of athletes, since communication must be by ski, by foot, and by hand-propelled boats? What more natural than that the buildings should be good, since the mistakes of the

[1] In this book place-names are usually given in their Finnish form, the Swedish form being added in brackets in the first instance; for, though English readers are no doubt more familiar with the Swedish form, the Finnish names are likely to be generally used in the future.

past, being made in wood, are all burned down and the monuments to the present have had to be hewn out of granite, a medium which is a discipline in itself? (*"Oui, l'œuvre sort plus belle d'une forme au travail Rebelle. . . ."*) What more natural than that music should be a living tradition, since the endless northern evenings left the people no recreation but singing? The economist too would have his answer pat if he were interested in cultural questions, but he would no doubt prefer to explain Finland's success in retaining democratic institutions. There have been Communist risings in Finland as everywhere else, but these have failed because the Finnish industries—wood manufacture and dairy produce—do not demand the concentration of a proletariat in large towns; the population of Helsinki, the largest, is to-day not much more than a quarter of a million. Therefore the workers of this northern world have never succeeded in uniting, and parliamentary democracy has persisted after its collapse in Russia, Poland, Germany, Italy, Spain, *et cetera*. The economist would add that there are troubles in store for Finland: her recent prosperity has been built on a constantly increasing demand for wood products of every sort from unseasoned timber to newsprint and cellulose; it will only need a drop in the world prices of these articles to plunge her into chaos. The sociologist would be less glib in his answers, but would doubtless suggest that most of Finland's achievements can be explained by the extraordinary balance that has been maintained there between the classes, between the races, and between the sexes. There is little conflict of interests between town worker and country worker; the smallholders are also wage earners, many of them going up to the lumber camps in the hard winter months. The industrial

19

worker has in most cases a relative with a farm of his own on which he can fall back in time of trouble. The rich are not much better off than the poor; in 1931 there were only twelve people with an income exceeding £6,500 a year, and the standard of living of the civil servants and professional classes as a whole was not much higher than that of the artisans. The conflict between the races, between pure-bred Finn and Swedo-Finn, has been minimized by centuries of intermarriage and the fact that they now enjoy a common standard of civilization. The conflict between the sexes, to use an old suffragette phrase, has hardly troubled a country where men and women have always worked together on the land. When the industrial revolution came it was natural that they should work together in the factories; 20 per cent of the industrial workers to-day are women, and all careers except the army, the navy and the ministry are open to them. Common tasks implied common privileges, and Finland was the first country in the world to adopt female suffrage.

The Finns themselves are more conscious of their short-comings than of their achievements. Pressed for an explanation, they would take their stand on the vague ground of national psychology. Zachris Topelius wrote of his compatriots: "The general traits of their character are: hardened, patient, passive strength; resignation; perseverance allied to a certain obstinacy; a slow, contemplative way of thinking; an unwillingness to become angry, but a tendency when anger has been aroused, to indulge in unmeasured wrath; coolness in deadly peril, but caution afterwards; taciturn reticency, alternating with a great flow of words; an inclination for waiting, deferring, living for the day, interrupted sometimes by unseasonable haste; adherence to the old and well-known, an aversion to anything new; attention to duty; law-abiding habit of mind; love of liberty; hospitality; honesty; a predilection for religious meditation, revealing itself in true piety, which, however, is apt to have too much respect for the mere letter. . . .

"The Finn is recognized by his close, distant, reserved attitude. It takes him some time to thaw and become intimate, but his friendship, when won, is to be depended upon. He is often too late, often stands in your way without noticing it; does not greet a meeting friend till he has passed him, keeps quiet when he had better speak, and sometimes speaks when he ought to keep quiet. He is one of the first soldiers in the world, but one of the last arithmeticians; sees gold at his feet, but cannot make up his mind to pick it up. Admiral von Stedinck said of him, 'The Finn wants a petard in his back to make him move.' In outward appearance the Finn is generally of a middle height and strong build, and his intellectual endowments want waking up. The awkward peasant boy is not to be recognized when he has gone to school for a year or two, nor the cowboy who was unable to count one bar on his birch-bark horn, but who to-day blows on a cornet in E-flat in Tschaikowsky's 1812 *Overture*. Vocation and inclination for work depend, in the Finn, on impulse. Per Brahe, the first Swedish Governor-General of Finland, said of him, 'It is to be noticed in this people who at home idle away their time on their stove, that abroad one of them works more than three other men.' Lastly, we must not forget, among their general traits of character, their love of songs, proverbs, riddles, exercises of thought and a disposition for satire which mercilessly ridicules their own follies and those of others."

In this book no explanations will be attempted. *Je ne suppose rien, je n'impose rien, j'expose;* and if, in the course of exposition, some of the more pressing social questions of our age are posed in connection with one of the diminishing number of countries which Englishmen can still view without spectacles tinted with partisanship, it will perhaps be well.

CHAPTER 2

THE FINNS AND THE SWEDES

"Oma maa mansikka, muu maa mustikka."
(My country is a strawberry, other countries are bilberries.)
FINNISH PROVERB

"Iagh war med landett och landett med mig wääl tillfreds."
PER BRAHE

THE story begins with the arrival of the Finns in the first century of the Christian era. Who the Finns are we do not know: all that can be said with any certainty is that they are a race apart, being related to neither Teutons, Slavs nor Mongols. Whence they came originally is equally doubtful. It is supposed that they began their wanderings from the lands between the Urals and the Volga. Some of them, known as Magyars, turned southward and continued their wanderings until eventually they settled in the fertile Hungarian plain. Others struck north and sending offshoots all over the steppes of northern Russia (there are believed to be two and a half million people of Finnish race in the U.S.S.R. to-day) journeyed on until they reached the country which is now Estonia. Here they came in contact with Gothic settlers who taught them how to manage cattle, how to grow rye, and how to build and sail a boat. And hence they made their way to Finland.

They came by two distinct routes, these first Finns: over the water and through the archipelago at the mouth of the Gulf to the country which they called Suomi;[1] or over the

[1] *Suo* = marsh. Suomi is to-day the native name for Finland.

swamp where seventeen centuries later Peter the Great was to build his northern capital, and round the shores of Lake Ladoga to Carelia. They came as hunters and trappers and made no settlements at first, but pressed on after their prey, driving before them the few nomadic Lapps who were the sole original inhabitants of the country. They made no attempt to till the scanty soil, though here and there they burned stretches of forests and raised a crop of sorts before moving on to put further stretches under the fertilizing fire.

At last the country yielded kindlier conditions. The immigrants found streams where fish were abundant and valleys where richer soil made permanent settlement possible. By the beginning of the eighth century there were three settled areas in Finland: Suomi in the south-west, Häme in the centre, and Carelia in the east. Each had a loose tribal organization of its own, and as time went on the life of hunting and trapping gave place to the more settled if not more secure existence of grazing and cultivating. The climate was hard and the soil thin. The family was lucky indeed which could get more than a few handfuls of grain to grow between the stones and trees in the four brief months of summer. Their settlements were separated by vast uninhabited reaches of marsh and bog and isolated by innumerable lakes. Yet the Finns survived and multiplied. In the struggle for existence they were victorious, and out of that struggle they forged a civilization which, if a poor thing by comparison with contemporary civilizations of the South, was at least their own.

They became adepts in all the arts which a northern people must learn. They felled trees and dressed the trunks into interlocking logs from which they built their single-roomed cabins (*pirtti*), leaving a hole in the roof through which the smoke of the fire might (or might not) find its way, and lining the rafters with spruce-boughs and moss for protection against the cold. They stripped the bark from birch trees and out of it made shoes and leggings, baskets, summer tents and boats. They cured the pelts of animals so skilfully that traders came from Frisia to barter salt for their furs.[1]

They became adepts too in the black arts, and it was from these that Finnish culture sprang. Their religion was Shamanistic; they believed in the magic power of the name —the magic sound that had power to bind and to loose. Those who knew the secret names, the Shamans, could work all miracles, they held the keys of the universe. The Shamans hid the Name in riddles and in incantations, and these the people handed on from generation to generation in the form of verses (or runes) which they chanted to the accompaniment of the five-stringed Finnish harp, a sort of zither which they called the Kantele. By the tenth century the runes had crystallized into metrical couplets of which each line had eight syllables. They were chanted by two singers sitting facing each other on the ground, clasping each others' hands. The leader sang the first line which stated the theme, the second developed it with a wealth of alliteration and repetition in the manner of a Hebrew psalm. Every singer elaborated and improvised upon the runes, weaving into them the stories of their heroes, Väinämöinen,

[1] The Norwegian Octher told King Alfred of a voyage he made round the north of Finland (circa 890): "The principall purpose of his traveile this way, was to encrease the knowledge and discoveries of these coasts and countreyes, for the more commoditie of fishing of horse-whales which have in their teeth bones of great price and excellencie; whereof he brought some at his returne unto the King. Their skinnes are also very good to make cables for shippes, and so used." (See *Hakluyt's Voyages*, vol. i, p. 11.)

Ilmarinen, Kullervo, Kaleva and others. We shall never know whether these heroes were actual men or mythical deities, but it is certain that there was in Finland a great verbal, traditional legend comparable to the Iliad of the Greeks and the Arthurian Legend of the Celts. It was the collection and transliteration of these legendary runes which, as we shall see, became the rallying point for conscious Finnish nationalism in the nineteenth century.

If there was one custom more than another which distinguished the primitive Finns from their neighbours it was that of the steam bath. Every *pirtti* was also a bath-house. In winter and summer alike every family regularly piled stones over the fire and heated them like pots in a kiln. They threw water on the baking stones till the cabin was dense with steam, and then climbed naked onto shelves set under the roof where the heat was most intense, and beat their bodies with bundles of birch twigs till the sweat streamed and the flesh tingled. The custom has survived to this day, though now a separate hut is built for the bath-house (*sauna*). Of its origin we have no notion, though Livy mentions a similar custom as being common among the Sarmates of Dacia.

In political ideas the Finns of the dark ages got no further than that of the tribe. Occasionally the tribes of the south-west and centre achieved sufficient organization to conduct a campaign against the Lapps of Pohjola in the north, though as time went on and the science of boat-building developed some were skilled and hardy enough to take part in pirate raids against the Swedish settlers of the Åland islands and against unknown foes over the deep waters beyond.

But it is probable that the Finns were more raided

26

against than raiding, for at a very early period vikings made their way across the Gulf of Bothnia. A few settled here and there along the rivers of Ostrobothnia, which is now the western province of Finland, but most of the vikings had no intention of exchanging one barren land for another: they pressed on to Holmgarth (Novgorod) and on to Kiev, which they conquered in the ninth century.[1] Finland they left behind them. The animation of an ideal was needed before the sporadic raids on that wild country could be galvanized into conquest.

That ideal was, of course, Christianity. The Latin faith had been preached in Sweden since the middle of the ninth century but it was not until the middle of the twelfth that a legate was sent from Rome to organize the Scandinavian Church. This legate was an Englishman, Nicholas Breakspeare, afterwards Pope Adrian IV, and his mission was extraordinarily successful. He called the first council of the Swedish Church in 1152, established new bishoprics, which he put under the primacy of the see of Lund, arranged for Sweden to pay Peter's Pence to Rome, and left the country under two of the most zealous servants of the Holy See that Scandinavia has ever known. The first of these was the newly elected King Eric IX; the second was an Englishman by birth, Henry Bishop of Uppsala.

These two men undertook to bring Christianity by fire and sword to pagan Finland. In the year 1154 or thereabouts, they led the first Swedish Crusade to Finland and forced the inhabitants of the district round Turku (Åbo) to accept baptism. (Whether or not there were any Christians

---

[1] The Finnish name for vikings (ruotsi, rowing-men) became applied in the form of Rus or Russians to the people of the principalities of Novgorod and Kiev which they conquered. Ruotsi is still the Finnish name for Sweden.

in Finland before their arrival is doubtful. Christianity was known in the Åland islands and modern Finnish historians believe that it was not unknown on the mainland; they suggest that Eric's crusade was prompted by an appeal from baptized Finns to save them from persecution by the pagans.) Eric soon went home; later he was canonized and became the patron saint of medieval Sweden. Henry the Englishman remained to organize the first Finnish bishopric at Turku. His death at the hands of an outraged peasant was not undeserved; but in later centuries Catholic Finns recognized Henry the Englishman as their patron saint. It is sad that we know so little about him. Legends cluster thick round his memory, but we have no direct evidence of him; the heavy-nosed blue-chinned effigy on his tomb is of much later date, and though the cathedral at Turku is a monument to his work no one can say how much part he took in its foundation.[1]

From this time onwards Finland became the battle-ground of the two warring states of Sweden and Russia (Novgorod) which were forming on her frontiers. Russians assisted the Carelian Finns to attack the Swedish settlement at Turku in 1240. To avenge this the Pope urged Earl Birger to lead a second Swedish crusade against Finland in 1249. The result of this second crusade was the conversion —if the word can be used for forced baptism—of the Finns of Häme, as that of the first had been the conversion of the Suomi Finns. It was Earl Birger who first established what could be called Swedish rule in Finland; the castle of Häme (Hämeenlinna) dates from his time. The battleground of Swedes and Russians now shifted eastward to Carelia, and

---

[1] See Dr. Tancred Borenius's article in the *Archeological Journal*, vol. lxxxvi.

in 1293 Torgils of Sweden led a third crusade in which he drove the Russians behind the line of the Neva and forced Christianity upon the Finns of Western Carelia. Thirty years later a treaty was signed at Pähkinäsaari (Nöteborg or Schlusselburg, the key to Finland) fixing the boundary between Swedish Finland and Novgorod.

No dramatic colonization or subjugation followed the Swedish conquest of Finland. A few Swedish peasants and traders came to settle in the coastal districts; a few Swedish grandees were granted Finnish estates where they became more of a terror to the Kings of Sweden than to their tenants in Finland. The Swedish crown was too weak to attempt any policy of centralization. Sweden was a loose federation of provinces rather than a unified state. Each province ("land") had its own laws and customs and recognized no rule but that of its own legislative assembly. Each province sent its "lagman" to elect the common king who took an oath to observe the provincial laws. The country of the Finns became a separate "land," Finland, and in 1362 a Swedish edict recognized its right to participate in the royal elections: "whenever a King shall be chosen, the judge shall come (from Finland) with priests and twelve men of the common people, to choose the King on behalf of the people."

The Finns were left to go their own way. Local administration was left in the hands of the Pirkkalaiset, or councils of the peasant aristocracy; the Pirkkala of the district where Tampere (Tammerfors) stands to-day were given the monopoly of Lapland trade, and the conquest and subjugation of the scattered Lapps of the Arctic region was achieved for the Swedish crown by the Finnish Pirkkalaiset. After the Union of Kalmar (1397) which joined

29

Sweden, Norway, and Denmark under what came to be Danish rule, the Finns were granted the right to issue their own currency.

The Swedish conquest proved to be a blessing to the Finns. It saved them from being overrun by the German Knights of the Sword who had enslaved the peoples of Livonia and Estonia. It saved them from being overrun by the Tartars who conquered Novgorod. It even saved them from the serfdom which feudalism brought to the countries of Western Europe, for the Swedes were a people of free peasants, and the Finns enjoyed the same liberties as the Swedes. At the same time Finland was brought by the Swedish conquest into the orbit of western civilization. From the Swedish settlers the Finns learned new crafts of agriculture and metal-working. From the Swedish lords they gained an example (not always edifying) of knightly honour and of knightly methods of warfare. And from a long line of Prince-Bishops of Turku (Åbo) they received the teachings of the Catholic Church long before the peoples on the southern shore of the Baltic. The court of the Bishops of Turku became the first centre of Latin culture in Finland. There was no academy for higher education, but Turku sent more students to the University of Paris in the century between 1350 and 1450 than any other northern see, and several of the Bishops of Turku— notably Magnus Tavast who died in 1450—were men of universal renown.

The most important result of the Swedish conquest is the least calculable. There is no way of measuring the effects of the intercourse between the two races. The sanguine, adaptable, extraverted Swedes intermarried with the phlegmatic, obstinate, introverted Finns and a third

race was born of the union, a race of Swedo-Finns who differed from either of their ancestors as widely as the Anglo-Irish differ from the Celts and from the English. The Swedo-Finns were to be found mostly on the islands and in the coastal districts and river valleys of the west. Cut off from the Swedes by the frozen barrier of the Bothnian Gulf, they could never be quite Swedish in outlook; cut off from the Finns by the even more formidable barrier of language, they could never be quite Finnish. The racial conflict was to play a leading rôle in the drama of Finland's history during the nineteenth century, but before that it hardly appeared on the scene; the people of Finland thought of themselves as homogeneous, neither more nor less Swedish than the people of other provinces that recognized the authority of the Stockholm Government.

It must not be imagined that Finland in the middle ages was any more or less civilized than other northern countries. The vast area of lake and forest remained sparsely inhabited by less than a hundred thousand peasants. Many of them had never heard of Christianity; they kept to their primitive Shamanistic culture. Most of them, huddled in their log cabins, had never seen a stone building; in all the land there were scarcely ten monasteries and not a dozen towns. Of these latter only Turku and Viipuri (Viborg) were really worth the name. The great cities of the north were Wisby, Reval, Novgorod; no trade routes passed through Finland.

The beginning of a new age in the Baltic was marked by the election of Gustav in 1523 as "King of the Swedes and the Goths." That incomparable ruler, who defied the imperialism of the Danes, the parochialism of the Dalecarlian peasants, the extortionate commercialism of the Hansards and the cosmopolitanism of the Roman Church, made Sweden into a nation in the full modern sense of the word. Thanks to the transformation wrought in Gustav's reign (1523–60) three new forces were brought to bear on Finland. The first was the Reformation which made Finland the Lutheran country which it has remained to this day. The second was centralized monarchy—does not the Swedish word *vasa* mean a bundle of rods?—which checked the development of any rapacious aristocracy in Finland. The third was the national warfare between Sweden and Russia for the mastery of the Baltic. The history of Finland during the sixteenth, seventeenth, and eighteenth centuries is largely the history of the action and interaction of those three forces.

The Reformation came to Sweden, as it came to England, primarily as a political measure. Gustav I confiscated the wealth of the Catholic Church and with the revenue of twelve hundred glebes founded a standing army. The spread of Lutheran teaching and the translation of the New Testament into Swedish came as an afterthought; they were largely the work of Gustav's friend and adviser, Olavus Petri, who had studied under Luther at Wittenberg. From Sweden the reformed Church spread to Finland. Here the clergy offered no resistance to the new doctrines, and Turku became a Lutheran bishopric without a drop of blood being shed for the old faith.

In truth the Catholic Church had struck no deep roots in its north-eastern diocese. It had founded no more than 141 parishes. A few Finns had found their way through Latin and scholastic philosophy to the rare atmosphere of Catholic culture, but in the process they lost contact with their own culture and so were powerless as proselytizers; and the foreign missionaries who came to Turku failed

33

before the obstacle of the most difficult of European languages. It was very different with Lutheranism. From the first it was grafted on to the indigenous culture of the people. The Evangelic faith was first preached in Turku by Särkilahti in 1523. The gentle Dominican, Skytte, whom Gustav I nominated to the bishopric in 1528 sent his most promising pupils to Wittenberg. One of these, Michael Agricola, studied under Luther and Melancthon for three years before returning to Turku to become rector of the cathedral school, in which post it was his duty to educate the first Finnish Evangelic clergy. Michael Agricola compiled the first books that were ever written in the Finnish tongue. He wrote an alphabet-book from which his people might learn to read, a catechism of the reformed doctrines and a prayer-book, and in 1548 published a Finnish translation of the New Testament.

So Protestantism became the first agent of popular education in Finland. Luther's hymn-book, the Bible, and the catechism were to be found in most households, and the first printing presses in Finland turned out more books in the Finnish than in the Swedish tongue. Children who were never to receive any other formal education in their lives came to the pastor for a few weeks' schooling in preparation for their first communion.

The same Reformed Church that made Finnish a written language made Christianity a living creed. As time went on more and more parishes were founded, and the long pilgrimage by boat and cart from the isolated farmsteads to the church in the centre of the parish became a national institution. Something in the northern soul of the people responded to the stern doctrines of the Reformed Church. Their old fatalism and deism merged with the new teaching in a way in which they had never done with Catholicism. Yet there was no violent break with the past. Skytte and Michael Agricola (Bishop of Turku 1554–57) were men of peace and lovers of tradition. Thanks to them, Luther's more violent words and Melancthon's iconoclastic teaching found no echo in Finland. The faithful still went to confession, the Host was still elevated, prayers were still said for the souls in Purgatory. "It was largely due to Agricola that the Reformation in the Church of Finland did not become in any sense revolutionary, but principally an internal reorganization of the National Church in an Evangelic, but at the same time a discreet spirit."[1] There is something very typically Finnish in this combination of religious enthusiasm with political common sense.

To take one concrete example of the easy transition from the Catholic to the Protestant religion. A few miles from Vaasa in the rich Ostrobothnian plain stands the parish church of Isokyrö, a simple stone building with a high-pitched roof lined with wooden shingles. The vast nave (100 feet by 48) was built in 1304 and the wooden rail and the pews in the tiny chancel cannot be of much later date. To-day two carved wooden effigies of the Virgin still stand on the chancel rails, though a single blow could have destroyed these frail Roman images. The early Catholic mural decorations have been painted out and in their place are line drawings in red, black and yellow wash. Nothing could be more vigorous and vivid and at the same time more homely and natural than these drawings, which date from 1560, in the first generation of Protestantism. There are three tiers of them, each six feet high, covering the entire length of each side of the nave. They represent Biblical scenes—the

[1] A. Lehtonen, *The Church of Finland* (Helsinki, 1927).

scourging of the money-changers, the last supper, and so on—the figures wearing the court dress of sixteenth-century Germany (or should we say Stockholm?) and having the rough features and heavy hands of Finnish peasants. Nothing incongruous in these Catholic statues and Lutheran murals seems to have disturbed the country people who flocked to Isokyrö church throughout the generations Sunday after Sunday.

If the Reformation came to Finland more or less spontaneously, the Swedish centralizing movement was applied to it as part of a conscious policy. While Sweden was entering into a struggle, first for national unity, then for imperial domination of the Baltic, the first Vasa Kings aimed steadily at keeping Finland a contented and loyal appanage. Gustav I in the course of a journey through the country in 1556 made Finland a Grand Duchy under his second son, John, and the Grand Ducal court at Turku during John's time gave the natives their first glimpse of lavish living.[1] There was considerable prosperity in Finland during those days if we are to believe the *Description* compiled by the Elizabethan George North from the writings of Sebastian Munster:

"Finlande is called a fayre countrye, because it is more pleasanter than Swecia. . . . Much wine is transported thither, out of Spayne, by the sea Balthic, which the people of the Countrye much desireth, onely to exhillerat their myndes. . . . This countrye doth excell Swecia, in corn and grain, both for plenty and goodness, because it is for the most part playne, and not so fenny nor hylly as Swecia is.

[1] Incidentally John was the only ruler of Finland who took the trouble to learn Finnish. He went so far as to send a diplomatic note in that language to the King of France.

36

There be trym townes in Finland, as Kusta, a towne fortified for the warres, Åbo their Byshops sea, Rasburg, Viborg, Karelia. Åbo is not far distant from Uplandia, Viburg is situated at the extreme borders and farthest boundes of all Fynlande, towards and against the Russes and Muschovites. It is the chiefe and principal place where theyr Soldiours and Garisons do lye, that defends and kepes those people from invadyng the Countrye. It is also a marte towne of great trafficke, whereunto the Ruthines doo often frequent. The Finnons have continual warres wyth the Muscovites in the arm or bosome of the sea Finnonicus: using in Summer the ayde of Shyppes, and in Wynter they combat upon the Ice. How populous was this Countrye and others lying about it manye greate and wyse men doo wytnes, as Methodius, Martir, Jordanus, Gothus and Paulus Diaconus, the which Aucthors do wryte that this people dyd swarme out lyke Bees. And they call these Northe Regions the Store house and Garnar of Nacions . . . the Inhabitants of Fynlande do speak two sundry languages. . . . Wherefore in many places their Preachers doo preache and interpretate the Scriptures in both tongues."

The period between the great reign of Gustav I (1523–60) and that of his grandson Gustav Adolf (1611–32) was not a happy one for Sweden or for Finland. John married a Polish Catholic, and dynastic strife in Sweden shaded into a national and religious struggle with Poland. In this struggle the Swedo-Finnish nobles took the part of Sigismund of Poland, hoping to obtain from him the right to mulct the peasantry which was traditionally denied to them by the Swedish Kings. The leader of these nobles was Klas Fleming who, though he held the position of Swedish Viceroy in Finland, had never learned to speak Swedish and was hated and despised by the nobility in Sweden. He kept in arms a large body of troops which he intended to use on Sigismund's behalf, and billeted them and their horses on the Finnish peasantry. The latter sent a spirited protest to Stockholm, and when no help was forthcoming they rose in arms against Fleming in the Club War of 1596. This Club War, like the sixteenth-century peasants' revolts all over Europe, was drowned in blood, but its results were not altogether negative. Charles of Sweden took his revenge on Fleming and decapitated a great number of the Finnish nobles, replacing them by a new stock from Sweden.

Better days dawned with the reign of Gustav Adolf and the long chancellorship (1612–54) of Axel Oxenstierna. To the tolerant foresight of these two men and of Per Brahe, the people of Finland owe many institutions which served as the scaffolding of their public life and the safeguard of their liberties until well on in the nineteenth century. Their Court of Appeal was founded in 1623 at Turku, where the King's Justice was administered in a manner more favourable to the peasants than to the local nobility. Their university was founded in the same city in 1640. Their towns were given charters under the excellent governor-generalship of Per Brahe (1637–40 and 1648–54). Their right to send delegates to the Swedish Diet (Riksdag) was strengthened by the organic law of 1617, which organized that assembly in four estates of nobles, clergy, bourgeoisie and yeomanry, to each of which Finland sent her quota. And if Finland was bled white for Sweden's wars during this century, if nearly a quarter of her men folk were fighting under Swedish colours, the wars were largely victorious and the colours were those of the finest army that Europe had ever seen. The conduct of Stålhandske's Finnish cavalry at Breitenfeld,

Nürnberg and Lützen is still the pride of their countrymen. Many of the heroes—some say one-third—of Gustav's armies were Finns who had adopted Swedish names and uniforms as the shortest road to glory (in both senses) in that age of Sweden's triumph.

Perhaps the chief effect of being part of a Great Power was the widening of the class cleavage. The race of Swedo-Finns was increased by grants of land to victorious generals[1] until by 1654 two-thirds of the land and nearly half the revenue was in their hands. After the middle of the seventeenth century, when there was little tolerance and less foresight behind Sweden's government, these soldier-nobles became a ruling caste. Instead of being the servants of a benevolent ruler they were left free to develop as an irresponsible aristocracy. They quashed the old democratic parish councils, whose power they transferred to themselves as provincial governors. They oppressed the yeomen-farmers until these freeholders were reduced to tenants owing rent in labour and kind to landlords who were often absentees. Attracted by the rising prestige of Sweden they became more Swedish and less Finnish in outlook; the aristocrats who had spoken Finnish in the sixteenth century and to some extent in the seventeenth, thereafter spoke Swedish, and Swedish became the language of schools, law-courts and local government. Finnish, which the Reformation had made a written language, no longer appeared on paper except in catechisms and devotional manuals; it was reduced to the language of the uneducated masses. And Finland herself, which had provided both leaders and revenue to

[1] Incidentally they were not all Swedes by birth. One of the finest tombs in Turku Cathedral is that of the Scots soldier of fortune, Samuel Cockburn.

Sweden in the seventeenth century, became little but a battlefield and a forcing-house for cannon fodder in the Great Northern War with which the eighteenth began.

The wars between the new nations of Sweden and Russia were a source of unmitigated misery to Finland. She was the anvil on which the fate of north-eastern Europe was forged. From the time when Duke Ivan III took the title of Caesar (Czar) to the time when Czar Alexander I proclaimed himself Grand Duke of Finland, the country had scarcely more than a generation of continuous peace. Ivan III devastated Finland at the end of the fifteenth century, and though Gustav I dealt gingerly with the Muscovites whom in his wisdom he foresaw would one day establish a tyranny over the East Baltic, he could not prevent further invasions in the sixteenth. In the seventeenth century Sweden took the offensive and in 1617 added to her possessions a buffer-state of Kexholm and Ingria, but the offensive passed to Russia in the eighteenth. While that demented genius Charles XII was conducting his fabulous campaigns in central Russia, the troops of Peter the Great were ravaging Finland from Lake Ladoga to the Gulf of Bothnia. The struggle which we call the Great Northern War is called the Great Wrath by Finnish writers. It was ended by the Peace of Nystadt (1721) which gave Kexholm and Ingria and even the province of Viipuri itself to Russia.

At this period the fortunes of Finland reached their lowest ebb. She had given her blood in transfusion after transfusion to revive the military glory of Sweden, and Sweden had been defeated. Without that blood the hard struggle for existence on the farms of barren Finland could not be conducted. A famine in 1696 wiped away perhaps a third of her population—130,000 is the approximate death-roll—in starvation and its attendant diseases. In the following generation there was never a winter but left a hundred huts with their occupants frozen to death, and whenever a summer brought an untimely night-frost, crops rotted and a wider desolation spread. Wherever the Russian soldiers passed they requisitioned supplies and burned villages. It is said that the population of Finland had sunk to less than 250,000 in 1721.

After that, recovery set in rapidly. Twice during the eighteenth century Sweden provoked Russia to war—the Vasas, like the Bourbons, forgot nothing and learned nothing—but the wars of 1741–43 and 1788–90 left no lasting scars on Finland, and on the whole it was a century of steady progress. The drain of blood and talent to Stockholm dried up; the Finnish-speaking masses settled down to their business of wringing a living from the soil and the Swedish-speaking nobility settled down to their business of wringing rather more than a living from the masses. Sweden's line of strong monarchs had come to an end; she was ruled like every nation from England to Russia during this period by cliques of aristocrats. They were men of intelligence and rejected no new ideas which would bring money to their purse. In Finland the nobles enclosed common-land, forced yeomen to sell their holdings and become tenant farmers, settled new families on crofts on condition of their paying rent in the form of service. They brought in none of the improved methods by which landlords in England were doubling the yield of their land, but they increased the area under cultivation and the population of Finland multiplied. By the middle of the century it had reached half a million, by the end it was half as big again.

Meanwhile there was a stir in the stagnant waters of

commerce. It was in this period that the export trade in wood products which has become the basis of Finland's prosperity was first developed. Timber which throughout the ages was felled for fertilizer, fuel, furniture and food now was cut down for export. The first tar factories and saw mills were built and the little towns of Ostrobothnia attained the dignity of staples for the new trade.

The naissant prosperity kindled new ideas in the minds of Finns. A country parson, Antti Chydenius (1729–1803), was struck by the possibilities of the wood trade for Finland and appalled by the restrictions and regulations by which it was hampered; for the mercantile system of state-controlled commerce had reached its highest pitch in the Swedish Kingdom by the middle of the eighteenth century. A full decade before the *Wealth of Nations* was published he developed many of the ideas which we associate with Adam Smith. "A nation does not gain by engaging in many kinds of trade," he wrote, "but by working in those occupations that are most remunerative, i.e. in which the smallest number of persons can produce goods to the highest value." Like the English Philosophical Radicals after him Chydenius believed in enlightened self-interest: "Every one looks to his own good. This inclination is so natural and necessary that all societies existing throughout the whole world, base themselves on it. . . . Each individual tends of his own accord to that place and that occupation in which he best increases the national gain." We are reminded of the famous dictum of another parson, Robert Malthus, who, incidentally, had travelled in Finland: "By making the passion of self-love beyond comparison stronger than the passion of benevolence, the more ignorant are led to pursue the general happiness, an end which they would have totally failed to attain if the moving principle of their conduct had been benevolence."

Chydenius's *laisser-faire* ideas were a deduction from his belief in political equality: "No one should be the master of another, none the serf of another," he wrote, "all should possess the same rights, all the same privileges. When that is so, a citizen possesses all that he can ever obtain in a well-organized society. . . . In this the State is very like a pair of scales. If the liberty of one or several rises too high in one scale, it can never happen otherwise than by the sinking of the others too low in serfdom." Chydenius was not the only voice crying in the wilderness in those days. Bishop Daniel Juslenius developed a sentimental interest in the land of his adoption and wrote books to prove that the Finns were descended from the lost tribes of Israel and that the art of writing, amongst other epoch-making inventions, originated with them. His nephew, Professor Porthan (1739–1803), brought a more scientific spirit to the study of Finnish folk-lore and philology. Altogether there were signs in the eighteenth century that the educated classes were taking a new attitude towards the promise of Finland's past and the possibilities of her future.

The form that this attitude took among certain of the ruling classes was to be of the utmost importance. The Stockholm Diet had usurped the authority of the kings and now controlled the government of the country. Men from Finland sat in each of the four Estates of this assembly, but in each they were in a minority. They sat as Nobles, Clergy, Bourgeois or Peasants, never as representatives of Finland; consequently they were always outvoted on matters concerning the interests of Finland. This was particularly galling to the Swedo-Finn members of the Estate of Nobles.

43

They began to toy with the idea of Home Rule, meaning the creation of an autonomous state in Finland which would provide a buffer between Sweden and Russia and at the same time give the nobles in Finland a free hand in their own country. The Czarina Elizabeth suggested something of the sort during the war of 1743, but the notion was not taken up in earnest until a Swedo-Finn colonel, Göran Magnus Sprengtporten, made it his own.

The Stockholm Diet, which the Estate of Nobles virtually controlled, was as corrupt as it was powerful. A new king, Gustav III (1771–92), came from Paris determined to reform it. With the help of Sprengtporten and other Swedo-Finns he carried out a *coup d'état*, and in 1772 imposed a new Constitutional Law upon the Diet. By this the Estates retained the right of voting or refusing money but the power of summoning and dismissing them was vested in the King, and the three non-noble Estates were given the right of outvoting the Estate of Nobles.

Sprengtporten realized that he had backed the wrong horse: Gustav III was going to be a greater danger to the nobility of Finland than the Stockholm Diet had been. He went over to the Russian service. When Gustav called up the Finnish regiments for war against Russia in 1788 Sprengtporten induced the Swedo-Finn officers to mutiny. He went so far as to submit to the Czarina Catherine "A Proposal for the Establishment of the Balance of Power in the North by the creation of an Independent Finland." He wanted a "Republic of the United Provinces of Finland" under Russian protection, suggesting that Sweden should be bought off by the acquisition of Norway. The mutineers, known as the Anjala League, sent a message of the same tenor to Gustav.

Gustav III, probably the most successful as he is certainly the least known of the eighteenth-century benevolent despots, rushed back to Stockholm and imposed a new constitution upon the Diet. This Act of Union and Safety gave the monarchy full control of foreign affairs, though it left the power of the purse in the hands of the Estates. Armed with new powers he returned to Finland in the summer and (incidentally with Sidney Smith in his fleet) defeated the Russians and signed a peace with Catherine establishing the *status quo*.

The Anjala League crumpled up for lack of popular support. Its epitaph was written by Porthan, who wrote: "This foolish, criminal attempt is detested by all, excepting possibly a few windbags among our nobility who probably hope that they can transform their fellow citizens into serfs on the Livonian and Courland model." Home Rule was all very well for the nobles who would be the rulers, but it had no attraction for the masses. For them, in ages that know not democracy, one single tyrant must always seem preferable to a hundred.

Sprengtporten remained in St. Petersburg. He had an inkling that the ideal which the last great Vasa had neglected and the people of Finland had scouted, might yet find a patron in a Romanov.

CHAPTER 3

FINLAND UNDER RUSSIA

1809–98

"Swedes we are no longer; Russians we never can be; therefore we must become Finns."—ARWIDSSON

THE ideal of Home Rule for Finland might never have been achieved at all had the country not by an odd combination of circumstances become a pawn in the game of Napoleon. The Emperor was determined to shut the Baltic to British trade. For this purpose he made an ally of Denmark and opened negotiations with Sweden. Not unnaturally Sweden refused to take orders against her evident interests in a sea which she persisted in regarding as her own. Napoleon therefore determined to coerce her: at Tilsit he persuaded the Czar, Alexander I, to make war on Sweden, hinting that Russia might keep Finland as a gratuity.

The Czar waited for winter. He knew that surprise is the essence of successful attack, but there was no hurry. He knew that a hundred Russian expeditions had failed in Finland, but now there were three new factors in Russia's favour. First, Sweden was to be attacked by Denmark and Russia simultaneously. Secondly she was notoriously weak and her King, Gustav IV, a vacillating lout. Thirdly there was, as he knew from Sprengtporten, a feeling among the noblemen of Finland that their ends would be better served under Russian protection than under Swedish. Therefore

Alexander waited confidently until mid-winter when Finland lay bound by a hard crust of ice and snow which made the best surface for the transport by sledge of large armies and provision trains. On 8 February, 1808, without any declaration of war, but covering the nakedness of their aggression by an insolent white flag of peace, Russian troops crossed the border and marched through South Finland to Helsinki.

The Swedish military machine moved rustily into action. The septuagenarian General Klercker moved his Finnish regiments northward to Hämeenlinna (Tavastehus), leaving Helsinki confidently, for it was covered by the seven hundred guns of Sveaborg, the impregnable island-fortress with its garrison of seven thousand men.[1] Russia met this move by sending a second army over the Carelian lakes to cut off his advance to the north. It was a risky movement, involving long and highly vulnerable lines of communication. The defenders were in a good position but they threw it away by incompetence and treachery. Klercker's command was given to Klingspor, of whom his greatest admirers could only say that he was "a great noble and courtier." He turned tail and marched his men towards the Arctic circle as far as Oulu (Uleåborg), giving the excuse that he intended to wait for summer and the arrival of Swedish reinforcements. When summer came Sweden sent no help. She might have sent Sir John Moore and his ten thousand Englishmen, but after being kept kicking his heels in Scånia for a couple of months, Sir John took his expedition home in disgust. Sveaborg was under the command of Admiral Cronstedt, who was, according to a Russian

---

[1] Sveaborg, "the Gibraltar of the North," was built between 1768 and 1772 by Ehrensvärd. It is now called Suomenlinna, the Fort of Finland.

general, "naturally of an anxious disposition." He surrendered his fortress on 3 May before a shot had been fired or a pinch of hunger felt. The same Russian general notes that "The Russians had hardly enough troops to occupy it and to superintend the disbanding and sending home of the Swedish garrison. . . . The garrison at the time of its surrender amounted to 208 officers and 7,386 non-commissioned officers and soldiers."[1] When the Russian troops entered Turku, the capital, they met with a civic reception. Sweden's cause in Finland had been betrayed by the Swedo-Finnish gentry.

But the war was by no means over. There were still the Finnish rank and file to be accounted for. Centuries of warfare against Russia had indoctrinated them with hatred of the Slavs; they were peasants fighting for their land, serving in Swedish armies to save their fields and homes from Russia. In April 1808, even before the ice-crust broke up and left the country an impenetrable maze of streams and lakes, the Finnish troops turned and fought their own war against the invader. They were magnificently led by three subordinate commanders whose names must be recorded because Finland has written them high in her roll of heroes. Adlercreutz, while his commander was waiting for Swedish help, turned and defeated the Russians at Siikajoki and Revolahti (Revolax), near Oulu. Döbeln, leading his Björneborg Brigade, loosened the Russian grip between Tampere and the Åland islands. Sandels, using those guerilla methods to which the country was best suited, cut to pieces the Russian communications in the east and held his own against the redoubtable Barclay de Tolly. For five

---

[1] See *The Conquest of Finland by the Russians*, edited by General W. Montieth in 1854.

48

months these officers held their own against the Russians, winning six pitched battles, though they had but 12,000 men against an army which was reinforced from 16,000 to 55,000.

Yet when winter came again the Russians were still in Finland, and in greater numbers than ever. They drove the northern army over the Bothnian frontier, they drove Dobeln out of the Åland islands. From these islands, which Napoleon rightly called the key to Stockholm, they attacked over the ice to within a few miles of the Swedish capital. Throughout that second winter and throughout the second summer the war went on, until at last on 17 September, 1809, Sweden gave in and by the Treaty of Fredrikshamn signed away to Russia the Finland which had been Swedish for five and a half centuries.

Meanwhile Alexander had made his own peace with the men who were entitled to act as the spokesmen of the Grand Duchy. In March 1809, six months before the fighting on the frontier ended, he called a meeting at Porvoo (Borgå) of the members of the Finnish Estates who had sat in the Stockholm Diet. The settlement which he promised them was unique in the annals of conquest: for a lasting parallel we must look on another hundred years to the Act of Union between Britain and South Africa. Instead of annexing Finland to Russia, Alexander left Finland with an even greater degree of self-government than she had enjoyed under Sweden. The motives of Alexander—"sharp as a pin, keen as a razor, untrustworthy as sea-foam"—will always be inscrutable, but it is probable that, just as in 1807 he had come under the influence of Napoleon, he was acting in 1809 under the influence of another histrionic character. Luckily for Finland, Gustav Mauritz Armfelt was a Finn. After a career of devoted service to Gustav III and the cause of strong Vasa monarchy he had fled to Russia and, like Sprengtporten, had found a home there. For all his brilliance as a soldier and courtier Armfelt proved, as a statesman, to be both liberal and consistent—a rare combination. Prompted by him, Alexander at Porvoo made the following declaration:

"Providence having placed Us in possession of the Grand Duchy of Finland, We have desired, by the present act, to confirm and ratify the religion and fundamental Laws of the Land, as well as the privileges and rights, which each class in the said Grand Duchy in particular, and all the inhabitants in general, be their position high or low, have hitherto enjoyed according to the Constitution. We promise to maintain all these benefits and laws firm and unshaken in their full force."

The Constitution referred to was that of Sweden as reformed by the Law of 1772 and by the Act of Union and Safety of 1789. The powers herein reserved to the King of Sweden were now transferred to the Czar-Grand-Duke; Alexander, who was Autocrat of All the Russias, thus became a constitutionally limited monarch in Finland. The Finnish rump of the Stockholm Diet became the legislative assembly, and a new executive council was created with the name of Senate, which was divided into two committees, one with judicial, the other with administrative functions. A new administrative capital was built over the little port of Helsinki. As a link between the Grand Duke and his Duchy a Governor-General was appointed to represent the Czar in Helsinki, and at St. Petersburg a Finnish Committee and a Secretary of State for Finland were appointed to bring the recommendations of the Senate to the ear of the

Czar. The first Governor was Sprengtporten, the first Secretary Armfelt.[1]

The "people who mattered" were well pleased with the settlement. Finland had got Home Rule. There was no need to doubt the sincerity of Alexander's promises. He repeated them again and again, stressing the fact that Finland was to be regarded as a nation. In March 1810 he announced:

"From the moment that, through the Will of Providence, Finland's destiny was entrusted to Us, it has been Our aim to rule that Land in conformity with the liberties of the Nation and the rights assured it by its Constitution.

"The proofs of devotion the Inhabitants have given Us since the Oath of Fealty, which they tendered to us of their perfect free will through their Representatives assembled at the Diet, have only conduced to strengthen Us in that purpose.

"All the steps we have hitherto taken, with regard to the internal administration of the Country, are simply a consequence of an addition to that fundamental idea. The maintenance of the Religion and the Laws, the formation of a State Council in the Nation's midst, and the inviolability of the judicial and administrative authority, afford sufficient proofs to assure the Finnish Nation of its political existence and the rights appertaining thereto."

What more could Finland want? She had her own law courts, schools and university. She controlled her own customs, ports and postal service. She had her own Lutheran

---

[1] It is an interesting sidelight on the character of Armfelt, if not on the nature of the settlement, that in 1810 he was negotiating to make Finland a British protectorate. The idea was that Britain would be glad to make Finland her base for Russian trade and the Czar would be willing to surrender the shadow of sovereignty in return for substantial commercial advantages.

51

Church. In 1812 her precious Viipuri (Viborg) province was restored to her, after being under Russian rule since 1721. Her people were free peasants, though linked to an Empire of serfs. They were free from military service and were guaranteed the protection of the power of All the Russias. Only once during the rest of the century was the noise of gunfire heard on her shores—that was when a Franco-British fleet bombarded Sveaborg in August 1855, during the Crimean War, and forced the demilitarization of the Åland islands. The peasants could settle down to follow the paths of peace. No economic revolution, no Free Trade came in the first half of the century to increase the wealth of the nation—and in that their contemporaries in English villages would call them blessed. Their unit was still the family household that supplied almost all its own needs. In lean years when summer frosts destroyed the crops many died of disease, but yet they were fruitful and multiplied: the population increased from a million in 1815 to a million and three-quarters in 1870. What more could Finland want?

It is not easy to give a definite answer. On the surface the people were contented, but underneath there was a sense of *malaise* which penetrated the whole structure of society, taking a different form in each of its strata. Home Rule meant the rule of a tiny minority, the rule of the Swedish-speaking aristocracy. The Czar had given Finland to them. He was hardly to be blamed for that. As Ralph Butler says, "Alexander was under the impression that he had annexed a Swedish province. The culture was Swedish; the religion was Swedish; when he visited the country the language in which the Diet greeted him was Swedish. The peasants, he was told, spoke a barbarous tongue of their own; but for all

Alexander knew that might well be a dialect of Swedish, as Little Russian was of Russian. He was not interested in the matter. Very few persons at this time were."[1] The Swedish-speaking aristocracy benefited by his ignorance. They had a free hand in the administration of the country. They were not cramped by the fact that the Czars, contrary to the spirit but not to the letter of the constitution, refrained from summoning the Diet once between 1809 and 1863; a good deal of legislation could be put across in the form of administrative decrees by the Helsinki Senate. They were able to build up a powerful bureaucracy; there were jobs for all, and titles for the toadies. But something was lacking. They were cut off from Sweden which was the fount of their culture and in whose service so many of them had found perfect freedom. They could not graft themselves on to the culture of Russia. They were Scandinavians: they might learn the Russian language and even profess the Orthodox faith, but they remained foreigners in Russia; the whole Slavonic outlook was strange to them. It is a striking fact that while other non-Slavonic nobles, particularly the Balts, had no difficulty in making careers for themselves under the Czars, no Finlander attained any eminence, except perhaps in the Imperial army.

For the Finnish-speaking masses it was worse. They had found a sense of unity in the campaigns of 1808. Like every other people extending itself to the utmost in the stress of war, they had felt that everything would be different when the war was over. And everything was just the same, if not worse. They were at the mercy of the land-owning aristocracy. They could not understand the Swedish that was the language of their courts and of their local councils. They

[1] *The New Eastern Europe* (1919).

were a subject-race and the time was not far off when, for the first time in their history, they would become aware of the fact.

The *malaise*, though by no means intolerable, was profound. It was first diagnosed by the publicist Adolf Ivar Arwidsson who, angry at the subservience of placemen to the new regime, exclaimed in 1821: "Oh, to have a real Fatherland, to be a citizen of a State, and not a squatter in a mangy province governed by stupid asses and sly foxes!" To Arwidsson is attributed the famous slogan: "Swedes we are no longer; Russians we never can be; therefore we must become Finns." It was hard enough for Finns to realize that they were "Swedes no longer." As Sir Edmund Gosse wrote in *Northern Studies*, "It is very interesting to note how much of what is most notable in the history of Sweden has proceeded from this desolate and distant province, now hopelessly separated from the realm itself. In the annals of statecraft, of the church, of the war, and of the navy, the names of Finns are singularly prominent. In literature some of the leading writers in each century—Frese in the seventeenth, Creutz and Kellgren in the eighteenth, Franzen, Frederika Bremer and Zachris Topelius in the nineteenth—have been natives of Finland." What "to become Finns" would mean, it would take a hundred years for the public to realize fully. But intellectuals came to see one facet of it after another until at last the whole people saw it and Finland emerged to independent nationhood.

The movement towards nationalism was slow and the stages of its growth were the same, *mutatis mutandis*, as in other countries of Europe. First it took the form of a Romantic revival, secondly of a movement for popular education, next of a political and finally of an economic movement.

The Romantic revival had its roots in the University of Turku at the turn of the century when Professor Porthan was inspiring his pupils with enthusiasm for the history and potentialities of Finland. When Turku was burned down in the fire of 1827 and the University moved to Helsinki there was a group of young men who were determined to carry on his work. They used to meet in each other's rooms for discussion on Saturday evenings and came to be called the Saturday Society. Differing widely in outlook, training and temperament, they were united in the faith that the future of the country lay with the peasants. Their achievement was nothing less than a Finnish Renaissance.

The first member of the Saturday Society to become famous was Johan Ludvig Runeberg, the son of a Swedish-speaking merchant-captain from Ostrobothnia. He came to Helsinki as a teacher of the classics and devoted his leisure hours to writing verse. By 1839, if we are to believe Sir Edmund Gosse, "he was recognized as the leading poet throughout Scandinavia." Some of his works have been translated into English, though they are hardly of the type that bears translation. It is difficult for English readers to imagine how this academic poet, whose round bespectacled countenance is so reminiscent of that of Schubert, could have become a national hero. He spent the best years of his life as a schoolmaster in the little town of Porvoo, and he never learned Finnish well enough to write in it. Yet a national hero he certainly is. His historical reputation was founded on a collection of poems appearing in 1848, the Songs of Ensign Stål, which tell the story of Adlercreutz, Döbeln, Sandels and the humbler heroes who fought for Finland in the Russian war. The book rings with a note of national pride which had not been heard in Finland before. Its dedicatory poem, *Vårt Land*, set to music by Pacius, became the national anthem.

While Runeberg was making the Finnish people confident of their future, the work of making them proud of their past was being carried on by another member of the Saturday Society, Elias Lönnrot. He was the son of a drunken village tailor and worked in a chemist's shop in Hämeenlinna until he had enough money to go to the University. He read medicine and in 1833 obtained the post of district medical officer at Kajaani in northern Savo, near the borders of Carelia. But his life was hardly that of a physician: he spent most of his time wandering through unknown Carelia, living in peasants' huts where he played his flute and learned their songs and stories. Carelia had been subject to even fewer civilizing influences than the rest of Finland. Lönnrot found there a vast oral tradition of magic-rhymes and riddles, legends and festival songs. The idea occurred to him of working up the whole tradition into a poem on Homeric lines: "When no rune singer could compare with me any longer in his knowledge of songs, I assumed the same rights which, in my opinion, most of the other singers freely resorted to themselves, namely the right to arrange the songs as they seemed to fit best."

He called the epic *Kalevala*. It begins with the Finnish legend of the creation of the world, goes on to the story of how Väinämöinen, "old and steadfast," vied with the young Lapland hero, Joukahainen, for the love of Aino; then to the quest for the Sampo, or Holy Grail of Finland, which the smith Ilmarinen had forged and the dowager Louhi captured. The narrative is interspersed with bridal-songs and dirges, and there is a long digression to the story of Kullervo whose only love was for his mother, but the poem has a central theme in the triumph of Kalevala, the Land of Heroes, over distant Pohjola—of Finland over Lapland, it may be, or Gotland. It differs from other folk-legends for, as Andrew Lang said, "Among the Finns we find no trace of an aristocracy; there is scarcely a mention of kings or priests; the heroes of the poem are really popular heroes, fishers, smiths, husbandmen, 'medicine-men' or wizards; exaggerated shadows of the people, pursuing on an heroic scale, not war, but the common daily business of primitive and peaceful man. In recording their adventures, the *Kalevala*, like the shield of Achilles, reflects all the hope of a race, the feasts, the funerals, the rites of seed-time and harvest, of marriage and death, the hymn and the magical incantation."

The first edition of *Kalevala* appeared in 1835. Twelve years passed before five hundred copies were sold, but in 1849 Lönnrot published an enlarged edition and the work sprang into popularity. The year 1835 has now become a milestone in Finnish history, and *Kalevala* has been recognized as one of the great folk-poems of the world.

It has a peculiar, if trivial, interest for American and British readers because Longfellow, a great admirer of the Saturday Society, copied its metre and some of its themes. The following fragment is taken from a translation of some Finnish runes by Sir John Bowring:

> *"Song was then by song repeated,*
> *Rapture was by rapture echoed,*
> *Not a tenant of the forest,*

On his four feet hurrying forward,
On his little patties tripping,
But came hastening then to hear him."[1]

This appeared in 1827. Longfellow's *Hiawatha* was published in 1855.

For readers in Finland the publication of *Kalevala* was of real historical importance. Now for the first time their tradition had become a written tradition. Now the Finnish language could really be a written language. Lönnrot became Professor of Finnish in 1853; his task henceforth was to develop the language, to invent words to meet new needs, to generalize its uses into grammar and syntax. There was nothing academic about Elias Lönnrot—any account of his wandering life or a glance at the witty, restless face in his portrait should be sufficient evidence of that—but he settled down to an academic task and devoted the last eighteen years of his life to the completion of a Finnish-Swedish dictionary.

To give the impression that this Renaissance was based on a romantic idealization of the Finnish soldier and peasant would be misleading. One of the greatest works that it produced, Aleksis Kivi's *Seven Brothers*, is a novel describing the life of a peasant family of the early nineteenth century in colours as dark as the earth they tilled, as lurid as the blood of the animals they slew. Kivi was born too late for the Saturday Society and was too little of a litterateur to have had any truck with it. He was a Finn of Finns and the value of his book to the national Renaissance is that the faith in which it was written was a faith in the peasants, not as they had been or as they might one day be, but as they

[1] Quoted by McCullum Scott in *Suomi: Land of the Finns* (1926).

were. For which reason his work was not immediately popular.

Meanwhile another member of the Saturday Society had begun to work on a new problem. Although Finnish was the language of the vast majority of the people and although intellectualswere singing the praises of the Finnish heroes, there was in the middle of the nineteenth century hardly a single educated family that spoke the language. Indeed, they had no means of learning it: Swedish was the language of every secondary school in the land, except in the Viipuri province where some German was spoken; Swedish was the tongue of teacher and preacher, of magistrate and official; and Finnish, with its fifteen cases and its obscure syntax, could not be picked up in any casual way. Yet if Finland was to be a united country, if it was to be in any sense a community, if there was to be any means of contact between the masses and the educated classes, Finnish must be taught in the schools. That was the creed of Johan Vilhelm Snellman, the first and most famous of Finland's national reformers. "The educated class," he wrote in 1840, "has not the slightest interest in the physical or spiritual well-being of the masses. Who among the men running the country are touched by the misery of the rural regions? What university graduate cares to lift a finger for the education of the Finnish common folk? The mass of the people are turned inward because of long-continued oppression. They might possibly dare to find fault with the sheriff or a clergyman, but a governor is looked upon as a little god and a senator is considered a *ne plus ultra*. They have hardly ever had an interest in the commune, parish, province or country, or thought that conditions might be better. . . . The bulk of the nation can never be raised so long as Swedish remains the language of administration and instruction." It was Snellman who turned Romantic nationalism into a movement for education.

Snellman was born of Swedish-speaking Ostrobothnian parents in 1806. He studied philosophy at Helsinki, and travelled as a journalist in Sweden and Germany before returning to take up the post of headmaster at Kuopio in northern Savo in 1834. It is significant that the only position open to such a man in those days was that of village schoolmaster. He was a disciple of Hegel and believed that a national community was something greater than the mere sum of its members. From Kuopio he edited a weekly sheet, *Saima*, the first political journal in the history of Finland, urging the necessity of education in Finnish. His belief was that if the Swedish-speaking class were to give up their language "those coming generations will transmit their invented culture to the Finnish nation in a form which will allow that nation to share it, and in which it can be recognized as belonging to the nation. That class of society (the Swedes) which through history has handed down all the power in this country will then become what it ought always to have been, but has not been—the natural leader of the Finnish nation, and it will have gained what it now lacks—the strong backing of the millions."

Saima was suppressed by the Russian Governor-General, Menshikhov, and Snellman's way might have led into exile had not circumstances arisen which brought the education movement into international politics. The Industrial Revolution was finding its way to Finland and was beginning to turn it into a rich country. The possibilities of using the water-power of Finland for industrial purposes were first seen by a Scotsman, James Finlayson, who set up a cotton-spinning mill at Tampere in 1837. The discovery of a new process for pulping wood was made in 1860, and in the decade that followed the exports from Finland's wood-converting industries were increased five-fold. New means of communication to tap the industrial wealth were rapidly developed: the canal joining Lake Saimaa to the Gulf of Finland was completed by 1856 and the first railway from Helsinki to Hämeenlinna was opened in 1862. The country where progress had always been as slow as the growth of an Arctic tree, got caught up in the wheels of the Industrial Revolution in the eighteen-sixties.

Now that Finland was becoming a desirable prey, Sweden coveted her anew and tried to arouse discontent with Russian rule. The Czar Alexander II (1855–81) decided to counter Swedish propaganda by supporting the Finnish nationalist movement. In 1858 a Finnish secondary school was opened at Jyväskylä; it was the first state-aided secondary school in Europe. As the new Governor-General, Berg, said: "If Fennomania had not existed it would have been necessary to invent it." Snellman welcomed Russian patronage, and the first victory of his cause was in 1863, when on his advice Alexander issued a Language Edict by which Finnish became an alternative to Swedish in documents submitted to the district and municipal courts. Officials were given twenty years in which to learn Finnish, after which the proceedings of communal courts were to be conducted in the language current in the commune.

The movement for education in Finnish now merged itself into a political movement. As part of his policy of conciliating opinion in the Grand Duchy and as a means of raising revenue, Alexander summoned in 1863 the Diet which had not met for fifty-four years. He flattered the members by opening the proceedings in person and by following Alexander I's precedent of speaking in French instead of in Russian. In 1869 he ratified a new Constitutional Law by which the Diet was to meet at intervals of not longer than five years. There was nothing epoch-making about this Constitution: it perpetuated the Diet on the old basis of the four Estates of nobles, clergy, bourgeois and peasants, an agreement which had been admirably suited to seventeenth-century conditions but which was oddly undemocratic for the nineteenth, especially when it is remembered that the representatives of the peasants were chosen by a method of indirect election which left the last word with the landowners. But the spirit of change was in the air and the revived Diet became the instrument of some memorable reforms during Alexander's reign. A Liberal party was formed by Leo Mechelin who won the position of the most eminent statesman in Finland. A commercial treaty was signed between Finland and Russia and a tariff arranged which was highly advantageous to the former. Steady progress was made towards Free Trade and Finnish exports were opened to the outside world.

Behind this united front for reform a bitter party strife was developing. The burning question was whether the country should be Swedish or Finnish in culture. Mechelin tried to ignore the dilemma, but Snellman insisted that "if the Liberal party plainly recognizes that Finland's existence depends on this, that the Finns shall take the place which the Swedish educated class has held for centuries and still holds, then indeed peace is easily concluded. . . . All Liberal promises outside that simple and clear position are froth." Snellman was right: the dilemma could not be ignored. His own party, the Old Finns, under the leadership of

Yrjö-Koskinen, the first politician to learn Finnish, took an uncompromising stand: its programme was "Finland for the Finns." In opposition to this a Swedish Party was formed in the late seventies to defend the rights of the Swedo-Finns, who, it was insisted, were not only members of the educated classes, since nine out of ten of the Swedish-speaking inhabitants of Nyland, Åland and Ostrobothnia were humble fisher-folks, peasants or artisans. In 1885 the Liberals amalgamated with the Swedish Party who thus obtained a majority in the Estates of Nobles and Bourgeois. Controversy raged over the language question. The Swedo-Finns were in a strong position in the unrepresentative Diet, but the Fennomans gained ground steadily: Finnish was permitted for official correspondence in 1886, and in 1894, after a memorable debate, it was allowed in the Senate.

Meanwhile great progress had been made in popular education. In the sixties, when English children were still thrown on the none too tender mercies of the disciples of Bell and Lancaster, an elementary school system was built up in Finland by Uno Cygnaeus who was a disciple of Pestalozzi. He was himself headmaster of the first training college for elementary school-teachers founded at Jyväskylä in 1863. The new schools were intended not merely for instruction in the "Three R's," but for physical and moral training; they were intended to make the masses politically conscious as well as literate before the end of the century. By 1905 there were 125,870 children at school. The language question presented no difficulties in these elementary schools —the principle adopted was that instruction should be in the language current in the district—but it held up the development of secondary education. The Senate refused to allocate public money to Finnish-speaking secondary schools. The first Finnish lyceum in the capital was founded by private subscription in 1873. There followed a race between Swedo-Finns and Finns to open secondary schools. The controversy had the advantage of making higher education seem a most precious privilege.

Though divided by party strife, Finland was politically alive. By the end of the century all that was needed to unite her as a conscious nation was a little persecution from St. Petersburg. And for that she had not long to wait.

CHAPTER 4

RUSSIFICATION AND RESISTANCE

1898–1917

"Just this much they got out of me: what an axe gets from a stone, a borer from a rock, a stump from slippery ice, or death from an empty room."

MAGIC SONGS (Lönnrot's collection)

FROM the Russian point of view the position of Finland was an anomaly. Here was a country which was part of the Russian Empire yet not one with it; which acknowledged the authority of the Czar, yet not as Emperor but as constitutionally-limited Grand Duke; which expected Russian protection yet made no contribution to the Russian conscript army; a country which included good Baltic ports yet subjected Russian goods to a tariff; a country whose boundaries began a few miles from the Russian capital yet where the Russian writ did not run.

Alexander II had accepted the position and rejoiced in it. Alexander III (1881–94) pretended to do the same. He repeated his father's promises to respect the liberties of Finland. No serious breach of them was made during his reign, though his proposal to refer the reorganization of Finnish coinage, postage and customs to a committee in which Russians were in a majority brought an angry deputation from the Helsinki Diet to St. Petersburg, and the Commission he appointed in 1891 to "draw up regulations for the Provinces of the Grand Duchy" provoked the

65

resignation of Mechelin. Alexander III believed in the value of a contented buffer country on Russia's north-west flank, and to an extent he knew his Finland. His son Nicholas II (1894–1917) had no such illusions and no such knowledge. The St. Petersburg government during his reign fell under the influence of Constantine Pobedonostsev, the head of the Russian Church and the most able reactionary in Europe. He believed that the religious and moral values which he cherished could best be secured by Russian autocratic government exercised in the interests of the Slav people. Finland, according to Pobedonostsev, must be brought into line with the rest of Russia, and for this purpose a new Governor was sent to Helsinki in 1898. General Bobrikov had made a reputation as a ruthless administrator in the Baltic Provinces. With his arrival in Finland a new chapter began in the history of the Grand Duchy.

The first step in the Russification policy was an attempt to make Finland contribute towards the defences of the Empire. The Finnish army had been reconstructed by an act of 1878 fixing the peace-time strength at 5,600 with a reserve of 20,000, and making military service compulsory for the moderate term of ninety days spread over a period of three years; it was clearly laid down that this force was not liable to service outside the Grand Duchy except in the case of a small detachment known as the Guard. The Army Bill of 1898 changed all that by prescribing that Finnish recruits should be drafted to Russian units and that Russian officers should be set over Finnish units; the term of service was raised to five years and a reduction of the period was to be conditional upon a knowledge of Russian. In other words Finland was to lose her military independence.

The Army Bill was rejected by Diet and by Senate. Pobedonostsev decided to play a higher card. On 13 February 1899, Bobrikov returned from the meeting of a secret committee in St. Petersburg with the script of a manifesto which he asked the Senate to print forthwith. The Senate refused. After two days of angry meetings Bobrikov got a vote of ten senators in favour of publication to ten against; he gave his casting vote and on the 15th Finland learned the contents of the manifesto. It included the following sentence:

"While leaving in operation the existing regulations for legislation on matters of local interest which bear only on the needs of Finland, we have considered it necessary to reserve to ourselves the final determination of matters of legislation which concern the whole Empire." Finnish Bills were to be drawn up by a Committee of Russian Ministers including the Secretary of State for Finland; only if they concerned Finland alone would they be submitted to the Diet. So Finland was to lose her political independence.

The reaction of the people to this was immediate and astonishing. There was no disorder. The country simply went into mourning. The Senate sent a deputation to the Czar, the Diet sent a deputation to the Czar; neither was received. Then a protest of the whole nation was organized. The press being muzzled, the wires tapped and the mail censored, signatures to the protest had to be collected by messengers running the gauntlet of Bobrikov's agents. In spite of these obstacles, in spite of the immense distances of snow and ice over which the inhabitants were scattered, 522,931 signatures were collected in two weeks from a population which could not have exceeded, in adults and children, 2,700,000. The protest was carried to St. Peters-

67

burg, without Bobrikov's knowledge, by a deputation of five hundred men representing most of the parishes of Finland. Nicholas refused to receive them.[1] He had taken his stand—or rather he had taken Pobedonostsev's stand—and nothing would shake him.

There followed a regime of calculated oppression in Finland. Bobrikov abolished all rights of freedom of speech and assembly. He attempted to enforce the Army Bill by calling up a batch of 25,000 conscripts. Of these 15,000 refused to serve. He could not imprison 15,000 men but he could and did banish seventeen publicists who defended them and dismiss fifteen judges who upheld their case. He replaced the Finnish police, provincial governors and mayors by Russians. He dismissed three hundred civil servants from their posts. He disbanded the Finnish Army and filled the barracks in Helsinki and other towns with Russians. And he made the teaching of Russian compulsory as the principal foreign language in schools.

It is not surprising that Bobrikov was shot dead (in June 1904). But it is surprising that no one in the Finnish educated classes seemed to realize that the Czar himself approved of persecution in Finland. The assassin, Eugen Schauman, a young civil servant, committed suicide, leaving behind him a respectful letter to the Czar of which the following is an extract:

"Since the Minister Secretary of State, whose duty it is to report to Your Majesty on matters concerning the Grand Duchy of Finland, is not a Finnish man, is not familiar with the laws and customs of the country, and has common

---

[1] Incidentally he also refused to receive an international deputation armed with a petition on the same subject, including among its thousand signatures those of Herbert Spencer, Florence Nightingale, Anatole France, Zola, Mommsen, and Ibsen.

interests with General Bobrikov, Your Majesty is not informed of the actual situation, nor as to what the laws of the land prescribe. Since there is no prospect of a truthful representation of the real state of things reaching Your Majesty within measurable period, and of General Bobrikov being in consequence thereof recalled, the only thing that remains is to act in self-defence and make him innocuous. This method is violent, but there is no other.

"Your Majesty, on the same occasion I sacrifice my own life by my own hand, in order to convince Your Majesty yet more fully what grave evils prevail in the Grand Duchy of Finland as well as in Poland and in the Baltic Provinces and in the whole Russian Empire.

"I have taken my decision alone, after mature deliberation. Your Majesty, in the face of death I swear by God that no conspiracy is connected with this. Alone I have taken my decision, and alone I proceed to action."

The truth is that the upper classes in Finland still trusted the Czar and on the whole accepted the necessity of Russian suzerainty. The thirty years of Alexander II's reign were the happiest they had ever known; the present persecution was a phase and would soon pass. One group, the old Finnish party of Yrjö-Koskinen, had even acquiesced in Bobrikov's regime: they meant to use this broom to sweep the Swedish section out of power for ever, believing that when the Czar saw the error of his ways they, the Old Finns, would come into their own. It was only gradually that a new party, the Young Finns, came into being to uphold a less opportunist policy. They drew their cultural inspiration from Germany, France and England, and took their stand upon law, declaring themselves supporters of the Constitution of 1869.

69

But the task of ridding Finland of Czarist persecution was not to be achieved by high-minded assassins or by legal-minded politicians. It was achieved by a policy of passive resistance, admirably timed and led by a new party representing an hitherto inarticulate section of the community.

The Industrial Revolution, which began in earnest in the sixties, upset the social balance in Finland. From time beyond memory the vast majority of the people had owned land. There were a few large estates, but their number was inconsiderable; the majority of the estates were small— fifty acres or so of cultivable land with perhaps five hundred acres of forest. The typical Finn was a yeoman freeholder.[1] He worked his own land, labouring in the fields for fifteen hours a day during the short intense summers and every daylight hour throughout the winter. His wife, besides caring for house and children, pig and cows, spun and wove the home-grown wool and flax, ground the home-grown grain and baked the bread. His sons and daughters were shepherds and milkmaids almost from the time that they could run. For additional help he relied on girls and young men who ate at the common board and lodged in the farm kitchen and barns until they married; then the farmer would give them a cottage with perhaps a vegetable patch and pasture for a cow in return for their labour on the estate. It was a patriarchal, almost classless system which relied for the harmony of its working on nothing more

[1] Unfortunately there is no satisfactory English word to describe this status. "Farmer" is inaccurate for it connotes a man who does not own his land; "small-holder" and "peasant-proprietor" besides being long-winded convey a misleading sense of poverty; "landlord" conveys an even more misleading sense of leisure and wealth; and "yeoman" is archaic.

ponderable than the strength and skill and good temper of human beings and on the regularity of the seasons.

As the population grew in the eighteenth and early nineteenth centuries an increasing number of younger sons asked the landlord-fathers to grant them strips of out-lying forest-land on which to settle. The landlords would make verbal agreements with these crofters (*torpparit*), arranging for them to contribute so many days' work and so much produce in return for their crofts. All went well until the beginning of the eighteen-sixties when a succession of cold, wet, almost sunless summers brought something like starvation to cottagers and *torpparit* and severe want to the yeomen. At that very time the Industrial Revolution set a new value on forests, the timber of which could now be sold at a good price to the saw and pulping mills. Not unnaturally the landlords began to refuse to grant leases to new *torpparit*. The result was the growth of a new landless class.

The lot of these wretched people was hard in the extreme. Some got taken on as labourers and were given a corner in the farm buildings and a place at the kitchen table; there was nothing to stop their employer from working them to death, and he had the right to punish them or expel them at will. Others who could find no work on the land shouldered their bundles and made for the towns to seek employment in the new mills. At the same time the existing leases of the *torpparit* were made more severe. They had no written agreements; there was nothing but humane feeling to prevent the landlords from demanding more and more work and more and more produce from the crofter until he was driven to abandon his *torppa* or sink to the barest subsistence level of living. Humane feeling often proved an ineffective barrier against the temptation of high timber prices, and the "*torpparit* question" became a vexed social problem by the end of the nineteenth century.

The status of the population in 1901 was roughly as follows. About 111,000 families—or a quarter of the whole —owned land. About 160,500 were tenants, of whom perhaps 68,000 were *torpparit* with farms of five to twenty acres, and the rest cottagers with a patch of land for potatoes or turnips. Below them were 207,000 families of landless agricultural labourers. It needs more than an historian's imagination to bring these facts to life; readers are referred to the *Seven Brothers* by A. Kivi, *Katrina* by S. Salminen, *Fallen Asleep While Young* and *Meek Heritage* by F. A. Sillanpää, all of which novels are available in English translation.

The population of the towns was then 12 per cent of the whole. It had grown faster than any other section of the community: in 1865 the urban population had been no more than 6·7 per cent. Conditions were no better in Finland than in any other nation in the first throes of industrialism: the sixteen-hour day was not uncommon; wages were no higher than the subsistence level; accidents were appallingly frequent (as anyone who has used a circular saw will understand), and the rest of the population was largely ignorant of the plight of the 80,000 mill- and factory-workers.

Among this urban community the seeds of a new movement germinated. It began by nationalist propaganda spread in workers' educational clubs by men of Snellman's persuasion, but later with the growth of Trade Unions transformed itself into a labour movement for better conditions, shorter hours, and higher wages. The workers were debarred from Parliamentary and local elections. Until 1895, when *Työmies* (*The Worker*) first appeared, they had no newspaper. Then, in 1899, the Labour Party was founded, with a programme including universal suffrage, the eight-hour day, and the improvement of the conditions of town-workers and of the landless agricultural labourer. Labour was beginning to distrust the nationalist movement; "this business of being patriotic," said one of its leaders, "is the mask behind which the vested interests parade on every occasion. If one accepts any view different from theirs, he is at once branded as a traitor of his country." The German Social Democrats had formulated a version of Marxism at their Erfurt Congress of 1891 and under German influence the Finnish Labour Party changed its name to the Finnish Social Democratic Party in 1903. Unlike the German party it looked beyond the towns for its support, for after the first few years half the members were drawn from the agricultural-labourer class. At first the party was very small, and though its growth was rapid (membership rose from 8,300 in 1902 to 13,500 in 1903) it is doubtful whether many people outside the employee class knew of its existence; and it is certain that no one suspected the part it would play in transforming nationalism from a movement of the educated classes into a movement of the masses.

In 1905 the collapse of the Czarist campaign against Japan brought hope to the persecuted all over the Russian Empire. There were revolutionary risings in St. Petersburg: it seemed likely that Czardom would be overthrown. In Finland the middle-class politicians felt vaguely that this was their opportunity, but they did not know what to do about it. The Social Democrats, on the other hand, knew exactly. They proclaimed a general strike. Trains stopped, telegraphs went dead, factories stood empty. This lead was followed spontaneously by the whole nation: shops, offices, schools, restaurants were shut. The police went on strike and the bourgeois university students formed a corps to maintain order: they wore white arm-bands and became known as the White Guard. Not to be outdone, the Social Democrats let their own young men wear red arm-bands and organize a Red Guard. There was no bloodshed; it was merely passive resistance with a whole nation behind it.

On the sixth day of the strike the Czar's ministers gave in. Witte sent a message announcing that Bobrikov's innovations would be withdrawn, that military service would not be demanded of Finns but a financial contribution accepted in its stead, and that the Diet would be summoned forthwith to re-establish constitutional government on a more representative basis. Before the year 1905 was out the Four Estates had drawn up a constitution transforming the Diet into a single House of Representatives. What is more, this House was to be elected by the votes of every citizen over the age of twenty-four, poor as well as rich, female as well as male. Thus at one blow the Finnish Diet made itself the most democratic parliament in the world.

The Social Democrats had won an unpredictable victory. Even more surprising than the victory was the fact that the leaders of the party did not pursue it too far. They might easily have tried to precipitate warfare between the classes, but they did nothing of the kind. It is true that some local branches of the Red Guard got out of hand. An ugly situation arose in July 1906 when Russian soldiers in the Sveaborg garrison rose against their officers and detachments of the Red Guard took it upon themselves to hinder the arrival of reinforcements sent from Russia to quell the mutiny. Finnish blood was shed: a party of Reds ran into some White Guards in a Helsinki square and shot seven of them down. But the Red Guard was soon disbanded. The Social Democratic Party refused to be distracted from its immediate work, which was the drawing up of a new programme at their conference at Oulu.

This programme of 1906 is worth describing in some detail if only because all except one of its eleven main demands have since passed into law. It was a programme of which English Liberals of that day might have approved. The Finnish Social Democrats declared at Oulu that they stood for (1) the right to nominate their own candidates for the Diet, (2) the right of the Diet to initiate constitutional reform, (3) civil rights for Jews, (4) universal suffrage in elections for municipal councils, (5) State aid for crofters, (6) an eight-hour day for adult workers and no night-work, (7) a five-hour day for workers between fifteen and seventeen and no work for children under fifteen, (8) an efficient inspectorate for factories, (9) State pensions for the sick and the aged, (10) Prohibition of alcoholic beverages, and (11) equal pay for equal work as between men and women.

To make sure of the support of agricultural workers for this programme they called a congress of *torpparit* which was attended by 400 delegates representing some 50,000 crofters of varying condition. It was the first time that *torpparit* had met to voice their grievances collectively. They elaborated in detail the fifth point in the Oulu programme and promised their support to the Socialist Party.

Meanwhile the middle-class parties were busy preparing their bait for the popular vote at the forthcoming elections. The Old Finns, adopting the euphemism common to

conservative parties the world over, now called themselves
Nationalists; the Young Finns appeared as the Constitutional Party. A new party appeared in the lists, the Agrarians,
who claimed to voice the interests of the smallholders. These
three and the Swedish Party itself each put a number of radical
reforms on its platform. It was a surprise to them when
the elections of March 1907, the first to be held under the
new system, returned Social Democrats to two-fifths of the
seats. It was a larger proportion than Socialists held in any
other national assembly at that time. Eighty out of the two
hundred seats were won by the Social Democrats; the rest
were divided among the middle-class parties as follows: the
Old Finns won 58, the Young Finns 26, the Agrarians 9,
the Swedes 25 and the Christian Labour Party 2. The
members included nineteen women, divided equally among
the parties. (See diagram p. 107.)

The Social Democrats had not a clear majority. They
proposed legislation on every one of the eleven points in
their programme. Some got through the Diet, a few got
through the Senate, one or two were even accepted by the
Czar. But the net result of the efforts of three parliaments
in three consecutive years was meagre enough. The eight-
hour day was established in the baking trade, and a nine-
hour day in most others, with night-work and overtime paid
at 150 per cent of the normal wage-rates. The principle of
equal-pay-for-equal-work was accepted in the State schools,
the Post Office, and the Railways. The Diet voted compulsory schooling between the ages of seven and thirteen,
with free board and travelling expenses when necessary;
the Social Democrats had wanted schooling from seven
to seventeen. It passed a measure for accident insurance,
rejecting the sickness and old-age insurance proposals of

the Social Democrats. A more important measure was passed by both Diet and Senate, an Agrarian Bill commuting all menial service for money rents and providing for compensation for improvements made by tenants. To this the Czar gave his consent as a favour but not as a constitutional right. The Diet, led by the Speaker, Svinhufvud, very properly refused to accept assent given in this invidious form. As Rosalind Travers wrote in 1911[1]: "It would scarcely be surprising if the Finnish electorate had lost faith somewhat in parliamentary action, seeing that any Social Democratic measure has to make its way past a succession of increasing obstacles, like the three lions in the fairy tale—bourgeois parties, Senate, and the Russian Government; and that *all* measures without distinction of party are liable to be endlessly delayed 'on the Tsar's desk,' discovered invalid, or frankly and contemptuously rejected."

The truth is that Finland counted without the new regime in St. Petersburg, a capital in which means are often changed but ends remain disconcertingly constant. Pobedonostsev was dead but his mantle had fallen upon Peter Stolypin, who was determined to pursue by new methods the old policy of Russification. Bobrikov's methods had been flagrantly illegal, Stolypin's were more deadly because cloaked with a semblance of legality. It was not difficult for a lawyer to drive the proverbial coach-and-four through the Finnish constitution. Finland had got a representative legislature, but not a responsible executive: the Senate remained a body nominated by the Russian Governor-General. Stolypin saw to it that the Social Democrats never had a preponderant voice in the Senate. The relations

[1] *Letters from Finland.*

between Finland and the reformed Czarist regime had been left vague. Stolypin made sure that the strictest interpretation was put upon them. In June 1908 he prevailed upon the Czar to sign a decree putting the supreme control of Finnish affairs, which properly belonged to the Czar personally in consultation with the Finnish Diet and his Finnish Secretary, into the hands of the Russian Council of Ministers.

From one point of view Stolypin cannot be blamed. The Finnish Social Democratic Party had certainly helped the Russian revolutionaries in 1905, and some of their members were still in correspondence with them. There was every excuse for close police surveillance. But there was no excuse for provoking an insurrection by trying to impose a dictatorship; which was the policy eventually followed by Stolypin.

The second period of Russification began like the first with the question of Finland's contribution to the Imperial army. In October 1909the Czarist Government insisted that Finland should pay £400,000 a year into the Russian treasury in lieu of military service. Members of the Finnish Senate protested that the sum had been voted for three years only and was not intended as a perpetual grant. They were overruled and five of them resigned. These the Czar replaced by Russians. At the same time he promoted to the post of Governor a General Seyn, who was well known and well hated as an accomplice of Bobrikov in the old days. The stage was set for Russification with a vengeance.

In June 1910 Stolypin got the packed third Duma to pass an Act which is best described by a back-bencher's cry: "Finis Finlandiae!" On this it may be best to quote H. W. Nevinson, who had been a Special Correspondent in

Helsinki: "The Act, rushed through the Duma and accepted by the Imperial Council, removed from the jurisdiction of the Finnish Diet all matters of Imperial concern; and under matters of Imperial concern were included Imperial expenditure and taxes, military service, the rights of Russian subjects in Finland, the use of the Russian language, the execution of Russian sentences, public order, criminal law, public education, associations and societies, public meetings, Press laws and the importation of foreign literature, the Finnish customs, copyrights and commercial privileges, the monetary system, the post, telegraph, telephone, railways and other communications, navigation and the pilot service, and the position of aliens. Such was the interpretation of the Russian claim as expounded by the Russian Members of the Finno-Russian Committee appointed to examine the question in 1909, and on their recommendation the Act of 1910 was founded." In fact it was the February Manifesto of 1899 writ large.

The coup—for it was nothing less—produced protests from nearly every country in Europe, not least from France and Britain who had recently entered into an entente with Russia. Memorials of protest were signed by a hundred French Deputies and fifty Senators and by a hundred and twenty members of the British Parliament; a declaration was signed by nine of the leading international lawyers in Western Europe giving their opinion that this was a breach of Finland's constitutional rights; *The Times* declared that "the Finnish Diet can, legally, only be modified or restricted with its own consent"; and Liberal opinion generally was voiced by Nevinson when he insisted that "Whether governments wish it or not, the peoples of Europe are, in fact, developing into a community of nations. Treaties and

79

international sanctions such as those on which the liberties of Finland are based, can not be torn up without a shock to the good faith and security of the civilized world."

Finland met the blow with sullen resentment. The people had not the heart to repeat the strike which had been so successful in 1905; nor indeed had they the opportunity, now that the government in Russia was stable. The politicians were too deeply divided along lines of class and culture to present a united front in any but a defensive direction. In the Diet voices were raised in protest, notably the querulous lawyer's tones of Mechelin and the more virile notes of Per Svinhufvud, the Young Finn leader, whom an English traveller saw "massive, pale and stolid-looking as a block of granite"; but they were impotent. A Senate of Old Finns—the traditionally Russophile party—resigned rather than acquiesce and Seyn replaced them by his own sycophants. Twenty-three members of the Viipuri Court suffered trial by a Russian tribunal and imprisonment in a Russian criminal gaol rather than give a dictated judgment on a test case. Two-thirds of the Finnish pilot service resigned rather than accept control by Russian officials. All over the country there were gallant but unorganized and ineffectual examples of passive resistance.

Russification ran its course. Stolypin doubled the sum due from Finland as commutation for military service and confiscated, as a contribution towards it, twenty million roubles which had been deposited in the Finnish treasury for expenditure upon education, public health and defence. Seyn filled up the posts of civil servants with Russian placemen and the time-tables of school-children with compulsory Russian lessons. He condemned to savage sentences of exile men who dared to open their mouths against him—

Svinhufvud, for instance, was sent to Siberia. Five times he dissolved the Diet, only to see each new election return substantially the same house, with slight gains for the parties whose opposition had been most marked.

This second period of Russification was to continue from 1909 until the Russian Revolution of 1917. The fact that in spite of the heightened political consciousness of the Finns it should have lasted for a year longer than the first is probably accounted for by the fantastic economic prosperity of Finland during that period. Every year the wood industry threw out new branches: cargo upon cargo was exported of paper, bobbins and ply-wood. Processing industries developed, especially in textiles, with materials imported from abroad; Tampere (Tammerfors) was nicknamed "the Manchester of the North"—a striking misnomer for the cleanest industrial city in the world. The population was increasing at a rate which makes figures hardly credible (see page 195). The drift of families to the towns grew faster every year, reaching a pace with which housing and amenities could not be expected to keep level.

In the middle of this came the World War. Not a man was called from Finland, though it was part of the Russian Empire. The Finns were left to get rich. And rich they got, some of them, beyond the wildest dreams of avarice. Finland supplied the inexhaustible Russian war-market with every commodity that could be loaded on truck or ship, wagon or sledge or lorry. The first two years of the war were halcyon days for Finland's capitalists. There was nothing they could not sell—and at their own price. There was nothing they could not refuse to sell: in 1916 when the Allied blockade shut the Baltic and the Russian demand threatened to drain Finland of her foodstuffs, the Senate had the courage to pass a decree forbidding the export of them.

Prices soared and wages, of course, failed to keep up with them. In normal times the Trade Unions could have brought pressure to bear upon employers, but now Finland was flooded with workers sent from Russia to assist in the manufacture of munitions and equipment for the armies. Finns had to compete with cheap Russian labour. Resentment ran high in the working classes; it was reflected in the 1916 elections which returned one hundred and three Social Democrats to the Diet—a success which, however, was to some extent due to abstention from the poll on the part of some middle-class voters as a protest against the Russification policy. For the first time the Social Democratic Party had a clear majority in the Diet. It availed them nothing because the Diet was not summoned.

Meanwhile the St. Petersburg Government was tightening the political screw. After all, Russia was at war and Finland was a part, though a privileged part, of the Russian Empire. The Czar declared his policy in a decree of 18 November, 1914, which laid down, amongst other things:

"The transfer to the tribunals of the Empire of all cases relative to offences committed by civil functionaries in their service.

"The extension of the control of the (Russian) Ministry of Public Instruction to Finnish educational establishments and to the University of the Emperor Alexander at Helsingfors.

"The regulation of the monetary system of Finland with a view to making it uniform with that of the Empire—and—

"The participation of the Finnish treasury in the expenses of the Empire in addition to the expenditures occasioned by military defences and particularly, by its sharing of the expenses of the Ministry of Foreign Affairs."

The cumbrous machinery of the Russian War Office set about making Finland an outpost in the Russian defence system. Russian garrisons increased until Helsinki was as thick with troops as Cairo and, to quote a native writer, "the erotic successes of the Russian uniform exposed the community to dangers of a peculiar kind." Russian engineers and overseers set Finnish labourers to work blasting out the granite round the south coast towns to build fortresses against possible attacks from Germany. A German expert said afterwards that he had seen nothing to equal these defences, not in Liège, Verdun, Warsaw, Kovno or the Italian Alps. The people could not fail to see in them a Russian plan to enslave Finland rather than a means to protect her from Sweden and Germany.

In every country whether belligerent or neutral the effect of the World War was to accelerate the processes of history; everywhere it made patent tendencies that had before been latent. In Finland it intensified the movement towards industrialization; it widened the existing cleavage between classes; it exacerbated the feeling against Russian officialdom. It made the years 1917 and 1918 the crucial years of Finnish history, for the outcome of the World War was to be to cut Finland free from Russia as that of the Napoleonic War had been to cut her free from Sweden.

CHAPTER 5

THROUGH CIVIL WAR TO INDEPENDENCE

"Never before has this barren Finland been so dear to us as now."
FINNISH RED COUNCIL, 8 April, 1918

In March 1917 the first Russian Revolution broke out. The Czar was deposed, and in the place of the Czarist regime a Provisional Government under the liberal Prince Lvov was established in St. Petersburg.

The Provisional Government had an unenviable reputation for ineffective and dilatory conduct, but with regard to Finland it acted with extraordinary rapidity. Within a week of its establishment the Finnish Diet was summoned and officials of the old regime removed; the execrated Seyn was arrested and a man of well-known liberal outlook, Michael Stahkovitch, appointed as Governor-General in his stead; political prisoners were released from prison and recalled from exile—among the latter being Svinhufvud, the Nationalist leader. What the members of the Provisional Government intended by this is clear: they intended to restore Finland to the position of a contented and progressive state under Russian guidance, and they thought that this could be achieved by restoring the *status quo ante* 1908.

This would have been all very well if opinion in Finland had remained stable in the last twenty years, but it had not. The second period of Russification had taught the bourgeois Finnish parties not to trust promises from St. Petersburg.

They took as their text the statements which President Wilson was making about the rights of small nations to self-determination: "All well-defined national elements shall be accorded the utmost satisfaction that can be accorded them without introducing new, or perpetuating old, elements of discord and antagonism." The Social Democratic Party, which it will be remembered had a clear majority in the Diet thanks to the elections of 1916, were equally convinced that Finland must determine her own future, but they were not so anxious to cut the working-classes adrift from all connection with Russia now that that country seemed likely to develop along socialist and democratic lines.

The so-called "Independence Bill" of 18 July, 1917, which the Finnish Diet passed by a majority of 136 votes to 55 was an outcome of these views. This Bill declared that the Diet could not be dissolved except by its own decree; that "the Diet of Finland alone decides, sanctions and decrees the execution of all laws of Finland, including those which concern State economy, taxation and customs"; and that "the Diet decides concerning the executive power in Finland. For the present the higher executive power is exercised by the Administrative Department of the Senate, members of which department are appointed and discharged by the Senate." Thus the Diet appropriated to itself all the powers which the Czar-Grand-Duke had held under the old Constitution, except those of controlling foreign affairs and defence. The Swedish party would have deprived Russia of those as well, but the Social Democratic majority preferred to wait upon events: they had no intention of jumping out of the Russian frying-pan into the German fire.

The July Bill went a great deal too far for the Provisional

Government which was now dominated by Kerensky. Stahkovitch ordered the dissolution of the Diet, adding that new elections would follow in which the public would decide on the July Bill. Here he came up against the Administrative Department of the Senate, whose permission was necessary before a decree of dissolution could be published. This Department consisted of six socialists and six non-socialists. Their vote resulted in a tie and Stahkovitch gave his casting vote in favour of dissolution.

The people of Finland who were to be asked to elect the assembly which was to decide the future of their country were in no mood for calm deliberation that autumn. All through the summer they had witnessed scenes of violence. Wherever there was a Russian garrison the rank and file had risen against its officers: in Helsinki "which ever way you cast your eye you saw only wild, armed bands with the expression of madness on their faces, carrying revolvers in their hands and the swords of murdered officers by their sides."[1] Wherever there was a gang of Russian labourers there was a strike, the Russians bringing the Finnish labourers out with them and teaching them the revolutionary slogans of the soviets. The police force struck in the capital, and middle-class students formed a Protection Corps to take its place, donning white arm-bands in memory of the White Guards of 1905. The Helsinki Corps was linked up with a more or less secret organization which had centres in twenty-three different districts where its White-Guard nature was concealed under the traditional disguises of "Fire Brigades" or "Athletic Societies." Alarmed by this the leaders of the Trade Unions announced on 20 October:

[1] H. Soderhjelm: *The Red Insurrection in Finland in 1918: a study based on documentary evidence* (Harrison, 1919).

"As the bourgeoisie is now feverishly arming itself against the labourers in order to stifle their most important endeavours for reform, the leaders are of the opinion that in self-defence, and to provide against all contingencies, the labourers should immediately raise corps of Guards up and down the country." Bourgeois writers denied at the time that they were arming at all, let alone feverishly, but the truth came out in 1923 in a pamphlet (*Finland's Civil Guards*) published in English by the White Guards: "Happily enough, at the end of October and the beginning of November, the central organization succeeded in importing one shipload of rifles, cartridges, machine guns and pistols, altogether 6,500 rifles, 25 machine guns, 2,500,000 cartridges, 800 pistols and 5,500 hand grenades." These were landed in Vaasa by the *John Grafton*, whose Master was a certain John Smith. The Red Guard was armed more freely, thanks to the Russian soldiers who were now their comrades.

Meanwhile the elections had taken place and the result was that the Social Democrats lost their clear majority. Instead of 103 members out of 200 they had now only 92. The reason for the decline was partly that the ordinary peaceable Finlander was shocked by the strikes and outrages of the summer, and partly that the lead in the movement for independence had passed to the middle-class parties. The Social Democrats had put full internal autonomy in their programme and had insisted on the lawfulness of the July Bill. But here they were on doubtful ground, for if the July Bill was lawful then the old Diet had not been legally dissolved and no elections should have taken place at all.

When the new Diet met it was faced by yet another change of government in Russia. The October Revolution had taken place and the Bolsheviks were in power in St.

Petersburg. In face of this threat to their economic privileges and indeed to all that they held dear, the middle-class majority of the new Diet lost no time in cutting itself adrift from Russia. On 15 November the Diet declared that supreme power belonged to it in virtue of—and here the cloven hoof of Privilege showed beneath the skirts of Legal-mindedness—the Constitution of 1772. A fortnight passed and the skies did not fall and no threat of retribution came from Lenin in St. Petersburg. Svinhufvud, now President of the Senate, was emboldened to draft a declaration of independence, and on 6 December the Diet formally proclaimed Finland a sovereign, independent state. Recognition by the outside world followed quickly: it was accorded by Sweden, then by France, then by Germany (anxious not to be forestalled by her enemy), then by Norway and Denmark. The first nation to recognize Finnish independence was actually Soviet Russia; Lenin had reasons of his own for wanting Finnish autonomy to be taken seriously.

Finland was an independent nation, but what sort of a nation was she to be? Did independence mean that the poor people would be free to exercise their rights under a democracy to establish equality of opportunity and to guarantee through the state a livelihood for the meanest among them? Or did it mean that the bourgeoisie were to be free to exploit the working-class, free to force prices up and to keep wages down, free to make fortunes on the Helsinki Bourse as they had done in the last few years?

The time had passed when this question could have been settled by debate. From abroad the great powers of Russia and Germany were preparing to send whatever forces they could spare to turn the scale in the interests of their own ruling class and their own national policy. At home hooliganism had already paralysed the normal machinery for preserving order. The White Guard, stiffened by Finnish officers returning from service in the newly disbanded Imperial Army of Russia, now numbered 37,000. The Red Guard was being swollen by Russian Communist leaders and by thousands of Russian as well as Finnish labourers who had been thrown out of work by the sudden cessation of war orders, as well as by every ne'er-do-well who happened to nurse a grudge against society. The Social Democratic Party which had called the Red Guard into being could no longer control it. The leaders who for eighteen years had kept the party to peaceful, constitutional methods, could avoid violence no longer. As two of the deputies (Blomquist and Piisinen) wrote: "the Social Democratic Party had been invaded by elements risen from the underworld; it is they and the Russian soldiers who led it on the road to violence."

On the night of Sunday, 28 January, 1918, the Reds carried out a *coup d'état*. The Government buildings of Helsinki were occupied and orders were sent to each local detachment of the Red Guard to take over authority in its own district. On the Monday a Committee consisting of Kullervo Manner, the President of the Diet, Tokoi, the Chairman of the Senate, and Eero Haapalainen, the Red Guardsman and Chairman of the Trade Unions, proclaimed Finland a Socialist Workers' Republic.

Middle-class writers from that day to this have arraigned the Finnish Social Democrats for handing over the country to the Bolsheviks of Russia. It is true that they admitted Bolshevik agents to their councils and appointed a Russian, Svetschnikov, to the command of the Red Guard; it is true that they abandoned passive resistance for insurrection. But it is not true that they had any intention of sacrificing one jot of Finland's independence or even of imitating the methods of their Bolshevik friends. The provisional constitution which the Socialist Workers' Republic drew up contains no reference to class-dictatorship or to soviet administration. This document—and it is no more than a document for it never came into force—is interesting as the first socialist constitution in history. It provided for parliamentary government by a Diet consisting of the same number of members and elected by the same methods as before. Executive power was to be in the hands of a Prime Minister elected by the Diet and watched over by committees chosen by the Diet for that purpose. Provision was made for a referendum on the petition of one-twentieth of the electorate, and direct legislation could be made if a petition signed by 10,000 citizens was presented to the Diet. The only sinister clause in the whole document is one giving Russians in Finland the same political rights as native Finns, a provision which might enable Russia to swamp Finnish elections. On the whole it shows the Finnish Social Democrats to have been much closer akin in their ideas to the Viennese Socialists than to the Russian Bolsheviks.

The Social Democrats had intended a *coup d'état*; they found themselves faced with civil war. On 26 January four members of the Senate had left Helsinki for Vaasa on the Ostrobothnian coast. There the White Guard was being organized for war by General Mannerheim, a Swedo-Finn officer formerly in the Russian Imperial service. The Vaasa committee, insisting that it was the sole legal government of Finland, negotiated with Sweden and Germany for

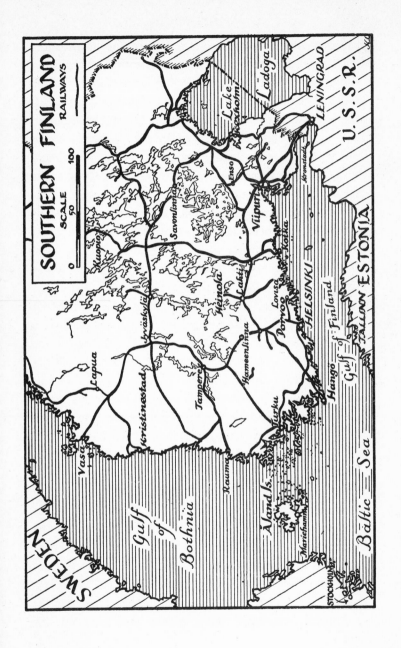

military support. It was joined by Svinhufvud who had escaped from Helsinki by way of Estonia and Germany. Mannerheim conducted raids on the small Russian garrisons marooned in the north and armed his guards with rifles and ammunition captured from them. Peasants began to enrol themselves in his ranks: to them it seemed that this was 1808 over again—another war to defend their holdings against the Russians who, whether they fought in the name of Czar or Commissar, were always Russians.

But the White Guard was not yet ready to fight: the officers necessary to train it as a fighting force were lacking. Luckily for the White cause these officers were at hand: on 28 February the first contingent of the Twenty-Seventh Prussian Jaeger Battalion arrived in Vaasa. The Jaegers were Finns, most of them students from Helsinki University who, abetted by their teachers in the darkest days of Russification, had made their way to Germany between 1914 and 1916. The German War Ministry had put them into a training camp at Lockstedt near Hamburg and allowed their numbers to reach two thousand before giving them a taste of active service on the eastern front in the 1916–17 campaign. The Jaegers, together with a few hundred volunteers from Sweden, supplied just the trained leadership which Mannerheim needed for his White Guards.

The Reds' northern capital was the industrial city of Tampere, situated on a spit of land between two lakes. It was the key to the railway system: if the Whites could only take it they would be in a most favourable strategic position. Mannerheim planned his offensive as a pincers-movement, intending to take Tampere with his Finnish army from the north while communications were cut from the south by a German army. For the Germans had promised help and had appointed General Graf Rudiger von der Goltz to lead an expedition to Finland. Svinhufvud met von der Goltz in Berlin on 12 March and it appears that they came to a close understanding, arranging for the Germans to land at Rauma whence a railway traversed direct the hundred miles or so to Tampere. But for one reason or another the sailing of the German expedition was delayed and the plan for landing at Rauma abandoned. On 20 March, Mannerheim, now in position outside Tampere, telegraphed via Stockholm to Berlin: "I consider it an urgent duty to hasten the arrival of the German expedition. Delay fatal." There was no satisfactory answer; Mannerheim had to undertake the reduction of Tampere without help.

While Mannerheim was building up a White Army at Vaasa and the Workers' Government was trying to organize a Red Army at Helsinki, the country as a whole was in the throes of revolution. In the villages groups of labourers wrapped red bands round their arms, and calling themselves Workers' Committees requisitioned shotguns and supplies from the richer farmers and co-operative officials and raided the houses of local worthies who were suspected of being in league with the Whites. Here and there the wealthier members of the community formed a White Committee and rounded up Red suspects whom they imprisoned in barns. On the whole the Whites predominated in the north and centre of the country; the railway line from Kristinestad through Jyäskylä to the Vuoksi could be said to be in their hands. Everywhere was uncertainty and indecision, for normal means of communication had broken down and no news of Vaasa or of Helsinki was coming through. The village committees had nothing but hearsay to guide them, and the rumour of a White advance from the north or a Red advance from the south was enough to precipitate a local massacre. In the towns there was the same uncertainty but less indecision. Except in the Ostrobothnian towns and in Kuopio, where the Whites predominated, the Workers' Committees were in power. Sporadic raids were made on the houses of politically-minded capitalists but neutral citizens, however rich, in most cases went unmolested, though they lived in terror and sometimes forfeited their lives by ill-judged attempts at flight. The Reds held practically the whole of Southern Finland; every important stronghold in the most thickly populated part of the country was in their hands, but they lost precious weeks trying to learn the elements of discipline and organization and the revolution passed on to the defensive.

The history of this civil war, like that of the Russian Revolution itself, has to be compiled from the wildly conflicting evidence supplied by belligerents. For the history of the siege of Tampere we are fortunate in having the evidence of a detached observer, Henry Laporte, a French financier who was escaping from Russia in the train of the Allied Diplomatic Corps and found himself trapped between the lines of Red and Whites; in *Le Premier Échec des Rouges* he has written a remarkable description of the siege of Tampere, which proved to be the turning point of the struggle. Laporte put his finger at once on the weakness which was to be the undoing of the Reds: their indiscipline —"le désordre destructeur, la naiveté, l'inexpérience." He tells how on March 21, when Mannerheim's admirably controlled forces were surrounding the city, the Reds ordered all men between the ages of eighteen and fifty to parade at nine in the morning in the Central Square; and at nine o'clock not a man turned up. Above all he foretold how the system of electing staff officers would be the ruin of the Reds. The elected Commander of the Red Army in the north was Salmela, a big, simple workman—"et le voilà promu, dans des circonstances critiques, qui exigeraient de grandes qualités de science, de coup d'œuil et de décision, au commandement des troupes maximalistes. Comment douter, après cela, que l'armée rouge ne soit inéluctablement condamné à la défaite?" Yet Laporte was unable to withhold his admiration of the courage shown by these untrained troops when the firing began. "Les Rouges font, ma foi, une très jolie résistance. Leur pertes sont lourdes, à juger par les blessés et les morts qui passent depuis deux jours sous nos fenêtres." It was 28 March, and women and children of twelve were going to the front now: "cette frenésie dans la défense a vraiment quelque chose de profondement emouvant."

March 29 was Good Friday and a heavy snowfall came to mute the battle. The Reds elected a new general, the young and energetic but totally unqualified Lehtimäki. On Easter Sunday the Whites refrained from sending over a single shot; they could afford to bide their time, for supplies were running short in the besieged city and the bread ration was cut down over the week-end from 100 grains to 50. At last, on 3 April, the assault came, beginning with artillery preparation lasting from 2 a.m. until the late dawn and followed by infantry charges which drove the Reds over the bridge into the square in the centre of the town. Lehtimäki drove up in an open car and flogged his men with the butt of a rifle until they went back to their positions on the bridge head, but his personal courage was impotent

95

against Mannerheim's generalship. On 5 April, Tampere fell.
Mannerheim took 10,000 prisoners.

The war was by no means over, for the south of Finland
was still held by the Workers' Republic. They had perhaps
90,000 men in arms against 60,000 or 70,000 Whites.
Fighting might have gone on indefinitely if help had not
reached the Whites from Germany. On April 3, while
Tampere was falling, 10,000 Germans under von der Goltz
were landing at Hanko and 2,000 more at Lovisa. This
force had been sent as part of the German campaign against
Russia, the plan of which was to detach from the Soviets
every province from Finland through the Balticum, White
Russia and Poland to the Ukraine. Von der Goltz' immediate objective was to crush the Reds in Finland and to
prevent the Allied force which was establishing itself in
the White Sea from effecting a junction with the Imperial
Russian fleet, now ice-bound in the Gulf of Finland; but
Germany's ultimate aim went beyond military and political
manœuvres. While the General talked of friendship ("*Die
Deutsche Freundschaft war sehr vielen Herzensache . . .*") his
compatriots aimed at economic penetration. Von der Goltz
himself tried to prevent this from being too obvious: "In
order to retain the newly-won friendship of Finland I must
again express the wish that German merchants and business
houses, in their natural desire to open new channels to
German trade, should refrain from looking on Finland as
an object of exploitation. They often fail to distinguish
between a prey and an ally, and there is a tendency to apply
to Finland, a poor and friendly country, the example of the
Ukraine which has just been secured for the needs of
Germany."

The Germans came in time to settle the fate of Finland.

The garrison at Hanko could offer no resistance; the Red
Guards were badly led—Haapalainen the commander and
Wesley his chief-of-staff were drinkers first and soldiers
afterwards. Von der Goltz pushed his way towards the
capital. At Karjaa (Karis) the Reds tried to hold him, but
without success. On hearing the news of this battle the
Red Government moved its headquarters from Helsinki to
Viipuri: "That was a proud time," writes the German
General in his memoirs, "when the mere appearance of
German steel helmets 120 kilometres from a strongly
fortified town accomplished the overthrow of a revolutionary government." On 12 April von der Goltz captured
Helsinki and on the same day the Reds evacuated Turku.
The Reds were now in full retreat towards the Russian
frontier. They found their way barred at the railway
junction of Lahti by a German detachment under Colonel
von Brandenstein. Here, sandwiched between Mannerheim's
forces and the Germans, 20,000 men were taken prisoners.
This meant the defeat of the Red cause, which finally
collapsed after some fierce fighting round Viipuri. On
May 16, nearly four months after the outbreak of hostilities,
General Mannerheim entered Helsinki in triumph.

The civil war is officially known to-day in Finland as
the War of Independence, the implication being that the
Whites fought for Finland's independence against Russian
Bolsheviks and the misguided native proletariat whom the
Russians had fooled into supporting them. This is the
view of Finnish writers such as Söderhjelm and Koistinen,
of Englishmen such as Sir Frank Fox and T. A. Atchley,
of Frenchmen such as J. L. Perret and Henri de Montfort
and of German and Swedish writers almost without exception. The truth, however, is not so simple. Actually each

side fought for Finland's independence as they saw it, and each side relied on help from abroad. Without foreign interference there could have been in the first place no war on any serious scale, and in the last no such rapid victory. The Reds asked the Bolsheviks for help: from Russia came stores and armaments. The Whites asked the Scandinavian countries and Germany for help: from Sweden came volunteers, from Germany came first Jaegers, then equipment, guns, and even aeroplanes, then soldiers and marines under General von der Goltz, then a fleet under Admiral Meurer. When the civil war was over the White politicians showed their gratitude to Germany in a fashion that boded ill for Finnish independence: they invited a German sovereign to reign over Finland.

This is one of the most curious episodes in Finnish history. In May 1918 the victors recalled the Diet, or rather they recalled 109 of the 200 members, for only one Social Democrat was allowed to resume his seat. This rump of a Parliament elected Svinhufvud as Regent, and Svinhufvud asked Kaiser Wilhelm II to put one of his sons forward as King of Finland. The intention was to set aside the republican constitution of December 1917 and then re-establish the old elective monarchy of Swedish days: so far Svinhufvud's policy is understandable enough. But why did he ask Germany to provide the ruling house? Was he fulfilling a bargain imposed by the Reich as the price of German help, or was he acting freely with Finland's best interests in mind?

The question cannot be answered until the German and British archives are opened to historians. Obviously Germany had political ambitions in the north. So, less obviously, had Great Britain, for the Government seems to have toyed with the idea of carving an independent Republic under British protection out of the Onega Triangle. General Mannerheim, who would have preferred British to German protection, resigned at the end of May. The best Finnish authority, Rudolf Holsti, then Finland's representative at the Allied capitals, suggests in the first draft of his memoirs that the General's resignation was forced by German pressure because he had formed a plan to occupy Eastern Carelia and to march on St. Petersburg in conjunction with the British Murmansk expedition.

Contemporary opinion outside Finland believed that Svinhufvud was acting under coercion. Sirola reported to the Russian Government that the German army in Finland had insisted on a German monarch. Haase, the German Independent Socialist Deputy, declared in the Reichstag: "What is happening in Finland is an indescribable tragedy: the Finnish people will never forget that agents in German pay called German armies into the country and let loose the most terrible of civil wars. Seventy-three thousand Finnish workers have been imprisoned, thousands of them have been shot *en masse*. Fifty members of the Finnish Diet have been arrested, and many of them have been put to death. The Finns have given to the citadel of Sveaborg the name of Golgotha. The man who governs with the aid of German troops, the dictator Svinhufvud, is responsible for these bloody orgies. He has already received his reward: he has been decorated with the Iron Cross." Balfour, the British Foreign Secretary, took the same view of German policy: "Consider her present position from the north of Finland right down to the Black Sea," he asked the House on 8 August, 1918: "She has gained it by the collapse of Russia. She has used it according to her own ideas. How has she used it? You have here displayed an admirable illustration of the way in which she pursues a single aim in different manner accordingly as the situation happens to direct her policy. The pose which she most affects is that of liberator; and I may incidentally observe that, next to being enslaved by Germany, there is no worse fate than that of being liberated by her. Finland, for example, is now being told that she owes her freedom to Germany! But Germany is plundering her, garrisoning her, choosing her form of government, and endeavouring to force her into the war."

On the other hand it must be remembered that Svinhufvud and his followers had no doubt that Germany was winning the war. Finland had been almost entirely cut off from the outside world: the only regular news that reached her came from Russia or from Germany, and news from Russia was discredited *ipso facto* by every White Finn, while German news naturally said nothing of the victories of the Allies or of the increasing weakness of the Central Powers.[1] In asking for a German monarch the Whites were putting Finland under the protection of the Power which was predominant in the Baltic; and this, after all, was Finland's traditional position.

The Kaiser refused the crown for his sons but allowed the name of his brother-in-law, Prince Friedrich Karl of Hesse, to be put forward. On 9 October, 1918, the Diet elected him King of Finland by a majority of 75 to 25. Prince Karl had spent an arduous summer trying to learn

---

[1] It is true that Rudolf Holsti sent dispatch after dispatch from London emphasizing the strength and resources of the Allies, but his reports were outweighed by those of Professor Hjelt, the elderly scientist who was Finland's representative in Berlin and who heard nothing but what the German High Command intended him to hear.

Finnish, but he was too wise to accept the offer out of hand. Unlike the Finns he knew that Imperial Germany was on the verge of collapse: on 9 November it fell and two days later the Armistice was declared.

The victory of the Allies was a piece of undeserved good fortune for the Finnish people. They had not expected it and they had done nothing to further it, but it saved them from a German ruling house and from the fate of becoming a German military satrapy—for whatever Svinhufvud's motives, there can be no doubt that Germany intended this future for Finland as she intended it for the Baltic Provinces, Poland and the Ukraine. The fall of the German Empire meant the end of German ambitions in the East and the withdrawal of Friedrich Karl's candidature. It also meant the fall of Svinhufvud who resigned the Regency on 13 November, hopelessly compromised by his pro-German policy. His place was taken by Mannerheim who had quarrelled with him at the end of May, holding out against the German rapprochement and urging the retention in arms of a strong Finnish army.

When all allowance has been made for foreign interference and propaganda, the struggle of January to May 1918 stands out as a civil war of Finns against Finns, the old Finland of yeomen and pastors led by the Swedish-speaking educated classes, against the new proletariat of the towns helped by the landless peasants. It was fought with the terrible brutality which is peculiar to class conflicts. During the war the Reds, it is estimated, put to death behind the lines and in cold blood upwards of a thousand men, mostly landowners and university students. After the war the Whites rounded up 80,000 men and women in concentration camps. Of these no less than 10,000, if we are to believe the official Finnish *Encyclopædia*, died.[1] These atrocities, committed by a race which has proved itself to be one of the most humane and law-abiding in the world, can scarcely be imagined by anyone who thinks of them by the calm light of peace-time. Every emotional state creates its own morality; what is good or evil in times of peace is not right or wrong in time of war. In the orgasm of their struggle for emancipation the Finns butchered and were butchered. That is all that can be said, though it may comfort readers who would find some excuse for the rulers who let 10,000 of their fellow-countrymen starve to death in prison camps to remember that there was a shortage of food in Finland and for the continuance of that shortage the Allies were responsible, since they forbade supplies—especially of American wheat—from coming in for fear of its reaching German troops. With the cooling of the passions of war, humane feelings quickly reasserted themselves in Finland. In the last months of 1918 over 70,000 prisoners were tried on political charges by subordinate courts and of these not 700 were acquitted, yet by March 1919 most of the sentences had been reduced and only in 125 cases was the death penalty actually carried out.

The civil war had cost Finland dear; the number of lives lost were believed to be 24,000. It remained to be seen whether national unity and independence were worth the price.

[1] See Jarl Hemmer's novel *The Fool of Faith* for a description of conditions in the prison camps on Sveaborg.

PARTIES IN THE DIET

Elections of	Swedish Peoples	Old Finns	Young Finns	Agrarians	Social Democrats	Communists	Fascists
1907	25	58	26	9	80	~	~
1908	25	54	27	9	83	~	~
1909	25	48	29	13	84	~	~
1910	26	42	28	17	86	~	~
1911	26	42	28	16	86	~	~
1913	25	38	29	18	90	~	~
1916	21	33	23	19	103	~	~
1917	21	32	24	26	92	~	~

		Concentrationists.	Progressives.				
1919	22	28	26	42	80	~	~
1922	25	35	15	45	53	27	~
1924	23	38	17	44	60	18	~
1927	24	34	10	52	60	20	~
1929	23	28	7	60	59	23	~
1930	21	42	11	59	66	~~	Fascists (I.K.L.)
1933	21	32	11	53	78	~	14
1936	21	34	7	53	83	~	14

not obliged to take their advice. The direction of foreign policy and of the armed forces is in his hands. He may call special sessions of the Diet and may dismiss the Diet at will. If the Social Democrats had had their way his position would have been very different; they refused to join the constituent Cabinet in April 1919 on the grounds that: "the Government shall not have the right of veto in regard to laws voted by the Diet and that the President shall have no other power than that which his right to vote in the Council of Ministers confers upon him. From the moment that the Government is responsible to the national representation, it follows that the Government has no right to dissolve the Diet." As it is, the President of Finland is in a very strong position; of all the Presidents of democratic republics only those of the United States and Czechoslovakia are comparable with him in power.

There are, none the less, definite checks on the power of the President. He has no authority over the Budget, which becomes law automatically after a single reading. All his decisions must be countersigned by the minister concerned. Further, these decisions are examined by the Chancellor of Justice; if this official is of the opinion that he is acting contrary to the Constitution he may indict the President before the Diet, where by a majority of three-fourths the President may be brought before the Supreme Court on a charge of high treason. In the ordinary way the method of presidential election should be enough to guard against dictatorial behaviour. The President is chosen for a term of six years by indirect election. The voters first choose an electoral college, by the same method as in a general election but to the number of three hundred instead of two hundred; the candidate who commands a majority in this college becomes President. Since no single party has so far been able to command a clear majority, the President has never yet been the nominee of a single party, but always of a coalition of parties, and therefore always something of a compromise candidate. Under most Constitutions this would be a disadvantage, but under the Finnish, which allows such wide powers to the President, it has much to be said in its favour.

Careful restrictions and the separation of power are, indeed, the keynote of the Finnish Constitution. The Cabinet is obliged to balance its budget and must get the consent of the Diet before raising a public loan. The Diet may not amend the Constitution without first going to the country in a general election, and then gaining a two-thirds majority for the bill. This procedure may be shortened only if the new fundamental law is declared urgent by a five-sixths majority of the House, in which case the election may be dispensed with and the amendment passed outright. The judges are appointed for life and a judicial officer, the Chancellor of Justice, watches over the legality of the conduct of Diet, Cabinet and President. Only in the financial sphere is there no separation of power, for the administration of the Bank of Finland is supervised by nine delegates who are appointed by and responsible to the Diet, the actual directors of the Bank being appointed by the Cabinet.

With its proportional representation borrowed from Belgium, its indirect presidential election borrowed from America, its main principles borrowed from England and Holland, this constitution may seem an unnecessarily complicated and cosmopolitan document, but in reality the fundamental features of it were already familiar to the

Finnish public. They had had a representative Diet of two hundred members ever since 1907. The extensive presidential powers were but a remnant of those which had been exercised by the Swedish kings. The judicial system remained unchanged: the old primary courts and the three Courts of Appeal remained, all that was added being a new supreme tribunal. The new document was in its essence merely, as its preamble stated, a development of the pre-existing Finnish constitution.

Such were the rules under which the political life of Finland was to be conducted; whether they would give free play and satisfaction enough to the various interests and aspirations of the Finnish people remained to be seen. Everything depended on the spirit of goodwill, without which the best Constitution in the world is no more than a scrap of paper and a sport for lawyers. The crucial question in that memorable summer of 1919 was that of amnesty for the people implicated in the Red revolt. The capitalist organizations—the Party of Concentration and the Swedish People's Party—were against amnesty. The middle-class organizations—the Progressives and the Agrarians—were in favour of amnesty: it was obvious to them that without it there could be no unity in the new Republic. When the Diet proceeded to the (extraordinary) election of the first President on 19 July the votes of the former were cast for Mannerheim and those of the latter together with the Social Democrats for Ståhlberg, the leader of the Progressives. So Ståhlberg was elected President by 143 votes to 50. A more moderate and at the same time able man than this ex-professor could not have been found to lead the Republic through the first six difficult years of its existence, but his election was enough to split the bourgeois coalition which had passed the Constitution. The Swedes went into opposition and a Progressive Agrarian ministry was formed under Professor J. H. Vennola. In December the first amnesty law was passed under which forty thousand people who had been implicated on the Red side in the civil war were declared guiltless and another three thousand were released from prison. At the same time the Social Democratic party pledged itself to parliamentary methods and expelled its communistic left wing.

The stage was now set for peaceful constitutional development. It was obvious from the outset that no single political party would be able to command a majority in the Diet. Nor would the two parties of the Right (Concentrationists and Swedes) or the two parties of the Centre (Progressives and Agrarians) be strong enough to form a Government. The only possibility was a compromise Government, a Centre-coalition depending either on the votes of the Swedish Right or on those of the socialist Left. Thus, Professor Vennola's ministry broke down in March 1920 because it could command the support of neither extreme. It was followed by a coalition under the Concentrationist minister Erich who maintained himself in power until he was succeeded again by Vennola after thirteen months. This was to be the average life of a Finnish Government in the first parlous decade of the Republic's history.

Nationalism the world over has three primary aims: to achieve self-government for a people of common race, language and traditions, to bring all outlying members of such a people under this government and to attain a frontier which will make its life as an economic unit possible.

Finland in 1919, like Ireland to-day, had achieved the

first of these aims, but not the second or the third. On every side her boundaries were undefined. To the north she had no outlet on the Arctic Ocean; to the south her territorial waters in the Gulf of Finland and her frontier between the Gulf and Lake Ladoga were not yet determined; to the east the future of the whole of Carelia was in doubt; and to the west her possession of the Åland Islands was disputed. These frontier disputes involved the issue which has been the most pressing throughout the whole of Finnish history: the relation of the Finns with Russia on one side and with Sweden on the other. It is to the credit of the leaders of the new Republic that they realized from the beginning that successful settlement would depend not so much on the extent of land they acquired as on their neighbours' contented acquiescence in the new boundaries; for only on the continued goodwill of Russia and Sweden could Finland's lasting independence be based.

The Carelian question proved to be the most difficult of these external problems. Superficially there seemed to be no difficulties. The Carelians, as we have seen, were originally akin to the Finns in race, language and culture, but the fortunes of war brought them under Russian influence instead of under Swedish. They were raided by Novgorod Russians in the eleventh century and were christianized by priests of the Orthodox Church; their territories were partitioned by the Treaty of Schlusselburg in 1327 and again by the Treaty of Stolbova in 1617. In 1809 when Finland came under the Czars, East Carelia was left outside the Grand Duchy: it remained an integral part of the Russian Empire and was treated as such. The Carelians remained serfs until 1861 and their condition after that was not notably improved. By the turn of the century there were but seventy-eight thousand of them, illiterate, impoverished peasants scattered over a land stretching from the Arctic Ocean to Lake Lagoda, from the White Sea to the Finnish frontier—an area as big as Denmark, Holland, Belgium and Switzerland combined. When the Czarist Empire fell in 1917 and the Bolsheviks promised the right of self-determination to the subject nationalities of Russia, there seemed every probability that the Carelians would declare themselves independent, or at least would become part of independent Finland. But one frail barrier stood in the way of such a simple and obvious solution. There had just been completed a ramshackle, single-track railway between St. Petersburg and Murmansk. This line which gave Russia an outlet to the Arctic Ocean was now the only open means of communication between Russia and the Allies. It was enough to bring Carelia into world-politics.

The fortunes of the Allies at the beginning of 1918 had reached their lowest ebb. The Italians had been crippled at Caporetto, the Americans had not yet landed troops in Europe, the Russian front had collapsed and the Germans were daily strengthening their western front with men brought over from the east. In this plight the British War Cabinet conceived a plan to reconstruct an eastern front so as to prevent Germany from bringing more reinforcements to France. With this purpose in view naval forces under Rear-Admiral Kemp were landed at Murmansk on the Arctic Ocean in March 1918, and in June General Maynard was sent with a larger expedition consisting of 600 British soldiers, 400 Royal Marines, a battalion of Serbian infantry and some French artillery. General Maynard was set a double task: first to prevent the formation of a German submarine base at Petsamo (Petchenga) or at Murmansk, secondly to co-operate with such Russians as were still pro-Ally in reforming a north-eastern front so as to tie up von der Goltz' men in Finland. He soon found that the British Admiralty and War Office had misinformed him on each point. There was no possibility of a submarine base being built at Petsamo: it was a miserable village with no harbour, no road to connect it with the interior and no railway nearer than 150 miles; even Murmansk would take years to equip as a naval base. Secondly there were hardly any Russians in the Murmansk area, and the handful that were there were not able or willing to fight against the Germans with whom Soviet Russia, since the Brest-Litovsk Treaty of March 1918, was at peace. It was lucky for Maynard that von der Goltz had not 55,000 troops, as the War Office had led him to believe, but 12,000, and that not one of these, as it happened, was ever sent over Finland's eastern frontier.

All Maynard could do was to attempt to induce the local people to defend Carelia against penetration by White Finns and Red Russians. For this purpose he organized a Carelian Regiment at Kem on the White Sea, and found a few hundred Red Finn refugees whom he enrolled in a Finnish Legion. Some topsy-turvy warfare followed. By remarkable sleight of hand Maynard succeeded in inducing Red Finns to fight against Red Russians and the Carelian Regiment to fight against their potential allies, the White Finns. By the end of October 1918 Northern Carelia from Murmansk to Kem was cleared of Maynard's enemies.

Then came the Armistice, and with it the whole situation changed. There was no longer any danger from Germany: most of von der Goltz' troops left Finland in the previous September. The *raison d'être* of the Allied expedition to Murmansk was gone. Maynard should have been recalled, but instead the forces under his command were increased. His task was now to win Carelia for the White Russians.

Who these White Russians were it is not easy to say. A puppet Government[1] of North-West Russia had been established by the British under the White-Russian General de Millar, who sent a certain Yermolov to Murmansk as his Deputy-Governor. Yermolov arrived on 5 November, a week before the Armistice was signed, and from that time forward the Allied expedition was a tool in Yermolov's hands. This quiet little Novgorod landowner persuaded Maynard to conscript the men of Northern Carelia into a White Russian Army and to conduct an offensive down the railway line so as to extend his recruiting area.

By June 1919 Maynard had reached the northern shores of Lake Onega. But that was the limit of his success. Already in February the Carelian Regiment had protested at being made a White-Russian tool. Its leaders declared that they were a non-Russian people and had a right to bring their claim for self-determination before the Peace Conference at Versailles. Maynard agreed that "at one time they (the Carelians) had been an independent race and the longing for independence was in their blood," but he had no sympathy for their aims: "Carelia," he remarks bluffly in his book *The Murmansk Venture*, "in fact was suffering from a bad attack of the malady known as swelled head." He disbanded the Carelian Legion, now four thousand strong, and impressed most of its members into labour battalions. At the same time his Finnish Legion mutinied under Lehtimäki and he had

[1] "I formed the opinion that the puppet government set up by us in Archangel rested on no basis of public confidence and support, and would fall to pieces the moment the protection of British bayonets was withdrawn."—Lieutenant Sherwood Kelly in the *Daily Express*, 6 September, 1918.

considerable trouble in getting the men disarmed and sent back to Helsinki before the end of the summer.

By now the Finnish Government had become highly distrustful of the Maynard-Yermolov combination. A Russian Carelia, whether White or Red, would be a danger to Finnish interests. The Finnish policy was to urge a plebiscite in Carelia in which the inhabitants might vote for their political future. In July an official note reached Maynard in which the Finnish Government offered to send regular troops to help him drive the Bolsheviks out of Carelia on condition that he would organize a free and general plebiscite.

Everything pointed to the creation of an independent Carelia when, in August, Lord Rawlinson arrived to superintend the evacuation of the Allies from the Carelian and Archangel areas. By mid-October the last Allied troopship had sailed from the Arctic area (leaving behind, incidentally, 327 British dead). Then events moved fast in Carelia. Yermolov's White Russians were soon wiped out by the Soviet forces. In January 1920 an assembly met at Uhtua, consisting of 124 delegates elected by the inhabitants of Viena (North Carelia): it voted unanimously "that Viena-Carelia wishes freely to manage its own affairs and to separate from the Russian Empire." The executive committee of the Russian Soviet Federated Socialist Republic countered this by calling a meeting in June at Kem, where 142 delegates, representing 24 out of the 45 Carelian parishes, approved the formation of a Carelian Soviet Commune.

The Finnish Government had by now given up hope of gaining Carelia, either as a Finnish province or an autonomous buffer state. Peace negotiations with Soviet Russia were opened and in October 1920 the Treaty of Dorpat[1] was signed. Finland recognized that East Carelia was part of Soviet Russia and gave up the frontier parishes of Repola and Porajärvi which she had held since 1918. Russia, for her part, recognized the Finnish Republic, gave up Petsamo and a narrow corridor to the Arctic Ocean to Finland and promised that East Carelia would have the fullest rights of internal autonomy.

The treaty was in principle and in practice a victory for the Finnish Government. Finland had gained an ice-free outlet to the Arctic: Petsamo to-day is a growing port, connected with southern Finland by the new (and only) motor road to the Arctic Ocean. And if she had abandoned all hope of Murmansk and of a White Sea port, if she had lost the East Carelian province, Finland had won the good-will of the most powerful of her neighbours. Now trade with Russia could be resumed, and the Finnish socialists who had sought refuge across the border could return to their homes secure in the knowledge that the new Republic was at peace with the Soviets.

Only the Carelians suffered. A Carelian "national" rising, which put three thousand men into the field against the Soviets in 1921, was suppressed without mercy. No free assembly was held. Members of the Russian Communist Party took control of the government of the province, which in 1923 was dignified with the title of the East Carelian Socialist Soviet Republic. Thus it became one of the eleven constituent republics of the R.S.F.S.R. which is itself one of the six constituent republics of the Soviet Union. The

[1] Dorpat is the old German name. Russians call it Yuiev, Finns call it Tartto, Estonians Tartu. Since it is now an Estonian city the official name is Tartu.

Communists have developed Carelia economically, strengthening the Murmansk railway, opening mines at Hiipina, cutting the White Sea Canal, increasing the population by immigration from Russia, but the Carelians are still a persecuted people. Finland tried to help them by bringing the infringement of the autonomy clauses in the Dorpat Treaty before the Hague Court of International Justice in 1923, but no decision could be given because Soviet Russia, then not a member of the League of Nations, refused to appear. Carelian separatists still hope that the League, or failing that Great Britain, will take up their cause. As the Academic Carelia League points out: "The Carelians themselves have been convinced that although they have had to endure the tortures of a Bolshevist hell for fifteen years chiefly owing to England's action, this cannot have been the intention of a country that supports the rights of small nations."[1]

When Finland made her peace with Russia in 1920 she was still quarrelling with her Western neighbour over the Åland Islands. These islands—about three hundred in all, with a population of twenty-seven thousand—are linked to the Finnish mainland by the Turku archipelago but are separated from the Swedish archipelago by a deep channel some thirty miles wide. Geographically, therefore, they are Finnish. Historically also they are Finnish, for they formed part of the ecclesiastic, judicial and administrative areas of Finland when that country was under Swedish rule, they formed part of the Grand Duchy of Finland under Russian rule from 1809 to 1917, and when Sweden recognized Finland's independence in January 1918 she tacitly admitted that Åland was part of Finland. But ethnographically the

[1] Akateeminen Karjala-Seuta (editors), *East Carelia* (Helsinki, 1934).

islands are Swedish: all the inhabitants speak Swedish (or the same dialect of that language which is found in the Turku archipelago) and there is no such uniformly Swedish-speaking area on the Finnish mainland. Furthermore the islands are strategically valuable to Sweden, for, as Napoleon remarked, "Åland is the key to Stockholm."

It was doubtless this last consideration which led the Swedish Government to fish in troubled waters during the World War. The islands had been demilitarized by the Peace of Paris of 1856, but this clause was waived by Germany in 1907 and by the Allies in 1914, and during the war Russia built a strongly fortified base in Åland. Not liking the sight of foreign guns so near Stockholm, the Swedish Government sent agents to play upon the pro-Swedish feelings of the islanders, and in August 1917 signatures were collected for a petition demanding the surrender of Åland to Sweden. Pro-Swedish sentiment grew warmer when the new year came and Red Guards from Finland began to take control of the islands in no ingratiating manner. There was a possibility that Åland detachments of the Finnish White Guard would hold their own in the islands but this was put out of the question in February when a Swedish military expedition made its appearance and sent the White Guards away to safety on the Swedish mainland. The Swedish Government insisted that this interference was inspired by humanitarian motives and that it did in fact save much loss of life. Finland's advocates, on the other hand, claimed that it was an excuse for Swedish occupation and that the White Guard were induced to leave Åland by a trick: they pointed out that the Swedes faked a message from Mannerheim urging the Whites to leave Åland and that a telegram from M. A. Gripenberg, the Finnish representative in Stockholm, was mutilated so as to read in the same sense.[1] However that may be, the Swedish occupation did not last long, for in May German troops took possession of the islands.

When the World War ended the question was still in dispute. There is no doubt that at that time the islanders as a whole wanted to become part of Sweden. Sweden was a rich and settled country, whereas the future of Finland was uncertain in the extreme, and every month made it more likely that the new state would be run in the interests of its Finnish- rather than its Swedish-speaking inhabitants. In this mood the islanders sent a deputation to the Peace Conference to urge their right to self-determination. The Conference referred the question to its Baltic Committee where, not surprisingly, it was pigeon-holed.

But Europe had not heard the last of Åland. In May 1919 the Finnish Diet passed an act granting a degree of local autonomy to the islands. This compromise did not satisfy the representative assembly of islanders which had been set up under Swedish guidance. It sent a deputation to Stockholm with the formal request that Åland be annexed to Sweden. The Finnish Government replied by sending a battalion of troops to Åland and having the members of the deputation arrested on their return. Relations between the two nations became increasingly strained; the Swedish minister was withdrawn from Helsinki and there was even talk of war.

At this point, in June 1920, the British Foreign Secretary brought the Åland question before the newly formed

---

[1] "Since it seems that your situation is untenable and that there is no hope of immediate relief, I strongly advise you to embark in the Swedish ships." The first half of this telegram was suppressed. See J. R. Danielson Kalmari, *La Question des Îles d'Aland* (Helsinki, 1921).

League of Nations Council.[1] The two nations were invited by the Council to state their respective cases before the meeting which was held in London. The Press reported the proceedings in some detail, and the newspaper-reading public all over the world heard for the first time of the existence of a Finnish Republic. The Swedish member claimed that the islanders had the right to self-determination and added, with some truth, that Finland was treating them with exactly the same disregard that Czarist Russia had once shown to Finland. The Finnish representative (Finland did not become a member of the League until the end of the year) insisted that the whole affair was domestic in nature and therefore for Finland alone to settle. This contention, though it had been the essence of Finland's case throughout, made the Republic momentarily unpopular with League supporters. The Council appointed a committee of three international jurists to examine it and the committee decided against Finland: in international law the Åland question was not of a purely domestic nature and therefore came within the competence of the League.

There were great rejoicings in Sweden, but they did not last for long. A second League Committee was sent to study conditions *sur place* and its report, presented in April 1921, pointed out that the Ålanders were but a tenth of the Swedish-speaking population of Finland and could not therefore claim the right of self-determination, which

[1] Under Article Eleven of the Covenant, by which "Any War or threat of War, whether immediately affecting any of the Members of the League or not, is hereby declared a matter of concern to the whole League, and the League shall take any action that shall be deemed wise and effectual to safeguard the peace of nations. In case any such emergency should arise the Secretary General shall on the request of the League forthwith summon a meeting of the Council."

applied to national groups as a whole and not to fractions of them. The Committee of Rapporteurs further concluded that the Åland Islands belonged by right to Finland.

The machinery of the League worked swiftly in those days. In June 1921 the League Council recognized Finnish sovereignty, adding that definite rights of local autonomy should be granted to the islands under international guarantee. Sweden accepted this decision with a grumble and Finland with delight. The Helsinki Diet passed a law ratifying the Constitution of Åland which is still in force to-day. The islanders have their own Provincial Council with definite rights of cultural and economic legislation, though the President of Finland has the right of veto and is represented by a Governor of his own nomination; they are exempt from military service; the state schools in the province may teach only in the Swedish language; and the Ålanders have a right of appeal through the Finnish Government to the League of Nations against any infractions of these safeguards.

This settlement would have been of little worth if Sweden remained unsatisfied, but her satisfaction was gained and her face saved in October 1921 when the League of Nations called an international conference at Geneva to consider the demilitarization of the islands. Germany, Great Britain, France, Italy, Poland, Estonia and Latvia were represented, as well as Sweden and Finland, and a treaty was signed guaranteeing that Åland would not be used for military purposes. Tension now relaxed as it was seen that every party to the dispute had won the substance of its demands. Sweden no longer had an armed enemy within her gate; Åland had a considerable degree of autonomy; Finland had retained her western province. At the same time the League of Nations had gained much-needed prestige by its first completely successful settlement of an international quarrel.[1]

Finland was now at peace with her most powerful neighbours. Only her relations with the new states of the Baltic remained to be defined. Poland had emerged from the war as an independent nation, and Lithuania, Latvia and Estonia, after being ravaged by Germans and Allies, White Russians and Red Russians, had also established themselves as free republics. Obviously Finland's fate was bound up with that of these other border-lands of Russia, but what was their relation to be? It was the opinion of Rudolf Holsti that they should be bound together in a defensive alliance. Four Baltic conferences were held between 1919 and 1921 and many minor projects of co-operation were accepted concerning postal, telegraphic and railway communication, patents, tariffs and commerce, but the major issue of a defensive alliance was not approached until a fifth conference met, at Warsaw in March 1922 (at which Lithuania was not represented, because of her dispute with Poland over Vilna). And then the scheme broke down through the refusal of the Finnish Diet to ratify it.

For the reasons of this refusal we must turn to the intricate stresses of public opinion in Finland. It is obvious that there were still many old sores to be healed before the Republic could play a healthy part in the new northern Europe.

[1] There is a vivid account of peasant life in the Åland islands in the novel *Katrina*, by S. Salminen, published in English in 1937.

CHAPTER 7

OLD PROBLEMS IN NEW FORMS

1922–28

"May the angriness of wounds dissolve like salt in the sea; the malignity of wounds sink like sand into water; may vexations melt like wax in the fire; may bitterness evaporate like dew on a sandy heath." MAGIC SONGS

IT is always surprising to find how little is settled by the realization of a political ideal. Finland had achieved her independence, but by that very fact many of the problems which had vexed her in the past were intensified. The mutual distrust between the Swedish- and the Finnish-speaking population, for instance, had been allayed by the common struggle for national independence but broke out in a more ugly form with the creation of the Republic. The Swedo-Finns were now terrified of being swamped by the Finnish-speaking majority, and they had every reason to be on the defensive. Most of the public posts and the best positions in business and in the professions were held by Swedo-Finns, yet the Swedish-speaking population of the Republic was no more than 10 per cent of the whole. Politically they were well organized, the bourgeois leaders of the Swedish People's Party never failing to command the votes of peasants and fishermen with whom they had little but the Swedish language in common.

The language question reached its highest pitch of

intensity in the months that followed the breakdown of the Baltic Pact, when a bill interpreting the language-clauses of the Constitution was before the Diet. The Constitution had prescribed that "Finnish and Swedish shall be the national languages of the Republic. The right of Finnish citizens to use their mother tongue, whether Finnish or Swedish, before law courts and administrative authorities, and to obtain from them records and documents in their mother tongue, shall be guaranteed by law, so as to safeguard the rights of both language groups in accordance with identical principles. The law shall provide for the intellectual and economic needs of the two groups in accordance with identical principles." It was round the interpretation of this phrase *identical principles* that controversy raged. To the rabid Swedo-Finns it meant "on a basis of equality"; to the more uncompromising of the Finns it meant "in proportion to their numbers."

Inevitably the bill that became law in June 1922 was a compromise. It made a distinction between unilingual and bilingual districts, defining as unilingual any district with a language-minority of less than 10 per cent of the inhabitants. On this basis there were in Finland, excluding Åland, 454 Finnish-speaking communes, 36 Swedish-speaking and 64 bilingual. Accordingly of the administrative districts one (Åland) became Swedish-speaking, four Finnish, three bilingual and one bilingual with respect to one commune only. The act provided that in all bilingual districts the public authority must use the language of the individual citizen with whom it happened to be dealing; and that every ten years there would be a new linguistic classification of districts.

Like every compromise this act antagonized extremists

of both sides. Controversy shifted now on to the subject of education, the ultra-Finns claiming that Swedish-speaking secondary schools had no right to more than one-tenth of the State grant. This cut at the very roots of their opponents' strength, for without superior facilities for secondary education the Swedo-Finns' cause would be lost. Luckily for them the ultra-Finns have never had their way; the State give 20 instead of 10 per cent of the secondary-education grant to Swedish-speaking schools.

Of all Finnish problems this language controversy is the most difficult for the outsider to understand. It is not a religious controversy: both parties profess the same Lutheran religion which embraces, nominally, some 98 per cent of the population. It is not a regional controversy: outside Åland there is no consolidated Swedish-speaking region; Swedish areas are scattered about in Finnish areas and the capital, Helsinki, which has a large Finnish-speaking majority, lies in a Swedish-speaking country-side. It is not a racial controversy: the Swedo-Finns have been born and bred in Finland and few of them can count a single purely Swedish ancestor for centuries back; many of them have no more Swedish blood than the ultra-Finns, being the descendants of men who learned the Swedish tongue and adopted Swedish names as the only road to advancement in the old days. Primarily it is a class struggle. The Swedish party is the remnant of the old ruling class defending its privileges against the Finnish-speaking *parvenus*. Because Privilege would make a poor party-cry they have adopted Swedish Culture as their slogan, and so have kept the support of the peasants in the Swedish-speaking districts, and of a number of intellectuals. But it is a difficult party to hold together on any but language questions. In fact the language quarrel in Finland, like the religious quarrel in Ireland, is an anachronism. The chief purpose it serves in this century is as a disguise for the economic conflict between the old ruling class and the new.

The language controversy pales into insignificance beside the real economic conflict, which must always be that between the Haves and the Have-nots. In Western nations where the majority of the population live in towns we are apt to think of this in terms of capitalists and urban proletariat. In Finland, where four people in every five still live outside towns, the conflict lies between those who have land and those who have none. In England the ambition of the average man is for a steady employment, with higher wages and shorter hours; in Finland his ambition is to own a plot of land where he can build his own house and farm-buildings and work with the labour of his family to wrest a living from the soil.

It was obvious, then, that the new Republic must stand or fall by its ability to satisfy the land-hunger of the masses. Of the 478,122 families who lived on the land at the time of the 1910 census, only 24 per cent were owners. About 33 per cent were tenant farmers and the remaining 43 per cent were agricultural labourers. Within each of these latter classes were two clear sub-divisions. Of the 160,000 tenant families, 66,500 were *torpparit*, that is holders of leases that could be revoked at the will of the owners. Of the 207,000 farm labourers, 84,000 held cottages and vegetable plots; the rest were landless. The problem before the founders of the Republic was therefore a double one: first to enable farmers and cottagers to acquire their holdings in full ownership, secondly to provide new holdings for the landless.

The first part of this task was broached in October 1918

by a law providing state loans for peasants who wished to buy their land. It was laid down that the price should be based on the value of the land in 1914. Owners grumbled that this was too low, land-values having increased since then, but they had seen something of the temper of *torpparit* and cottagers in the civil war of 1918 and in most cases they were not unwilling to come to terms with their tenants.

Little was done about the second part of the task until 1922 when circumstances made it of immediate importance. The Communist wing of the Social Democratic Party had broken away from the moderates and under the name of the Finnish Labour Party (the term Communist was illegal) had won twenty-seven seats at the 1920 elections. At the elections of 1922 the Communists retained their twenty-seven seats and it seemed likely that unless something was done to wean the masses from Communism the capitalist Republic must ultimately be overthrown. Agitators could point to Russia where the Bolsheviks had allowed the peasants to seize the land, and contrasted it with Poland where the new Republican Government preserved the vast estates intact. Revolutionaries who had no sympathy with communism could point to the new peasant Republics of Estonia, Latvia and Lithuania where the landlords were being expropriated to make way for hundreds of thousands of smallholders.

On the crest of this wave of feeling the Agrarian leader Kyosti Kallio formed a ministry in September 1922. He depended on the support of Social Democrats and Progressives as well as that of his own party and was pledged to find land for the landless. The problem was not so simple as that which faced the agrarian reformers of Estonia, Latvia, and Lithuania where the landowners were Baltic or

Polish barons and could easily be expropriated as anti-national aliens. The landowners of Finland were Finns; there could be no question of robbing them of their estates. A compromise was found in the bill which became law in October 1927. The *Lex Kallio*, as it is called, provided State aid for the purchase of two types of holding in hitherto uncultivated land. The first type consisted of small farms of a maximum of 20 hectares of agricultural land with another 20 hectares for firewood, the second type consisted of plots of 2 hectares maximum for cottage-sites and vegetable allotment. The landlords were to be paid by the State in Government 7 per cent bonds; the new landowners were to pay the State at the rate of 7 per cent per annum of the cost price, 4 per cent of which ranked as interest and 3 per cent went to pay off the capital debt; the new cottagers paid 9 per cent, a burden which being wage-earners as well as allotment-holders they could be expected to bear.

There was considerable opposition from the right-wing parties (especially from the Swedes who tried to pass an amendment forbidding the acquisition of land in Swedish-speaking areas by Finnish-speaking peasants) but it was overcome by the law's very careful limit on forced sales. Under the *Lex Kallio* expropriation became legal only as a last resort. In the case of estates of 200 hectares and under there could be no expropriation; in estates of 500 hectares the maximum with which landlords could be forced to part was 25 hectares; only in estates of over 500 hectares could expropriation reach the legal limit of 50 per cent of the uncultivated land. In spite of its leniency to landlords and the fact that it was creating that most conservative of social groups, a peasant-proprietor class, Kallio's bill was supported in all its stages by the Social Democrats. The

Communists, on the other hand, were loud in their opposition. In this they were backed by the Third International and by the Soviet Government—it must be remembered that those were the days when Moscow's policy was openly to ferment revolutions outside Russia. The connection between the Finnish Communists and the Russian became so close that during the parliamentary recess in August 1923 Kallio dissolved the "Labour" Party, shut its headquarters and its newspaper offices and arrested its leaders, including the twenty-seven members of the Diet. Then and only then, did the Social Democrats demur. When the Diet reassembled they insisted that Kallio had infringed the liberty of members and had rendered the Diet legally incompetent to legislate. President Ståhlberg did not share this opinion, but he took the view that since the Diet in its mutilated form was obviously unrepresentative a new election should be held. Kallio resigned and the Diet was dissolved. The elections of 1924 showed, as might be expected, a loss for the Communists (who had again changed their name to escape the penalties of the law). They retained only eighteen seats. The gainers were the Social Democrats and the Concentration Party; for the ensuing year the conservative Lauri Ingman was to be Prime Minister.

In spite of storms in political teacups the agrarian reforms worked smoothly. The Government used no force: it did not once have to exercise its right of expropriation, nor on the other hand did it find any difficulty in finding worthy candidates for proprietorship. By 1929 over 144,000,000 marks had been lent to purchasers of new estates, but never was a State loan spent to better purpose. The agrarian reforms were a success in three distinct respects. First the number of peasant proprietors was increased. By the end of 1934 some 65,000 leaseholders had become owners of land and another 53,000 had become cottage-and-allotment owners. By the same date under the Lex Kallio 31,000 new estates had been founded on hitherto unworked land, half of these being productive farms and half cottage-holdings for labourers. To-day one Finnish family in every three owns land: there lies the greatest difference between Finland and the older states of Europe. Secondly the area under cultivation was increased. In the first twelve years of its working the Lex Kallio brought over two million additional acres of land under cultivation. Thirdly the productivity of the land acre for acre was increased. Statistics are a poor way of measuring the Finns' growing skill in working the land, but we know no other. In the production of hay and animal fodder (Finland's chief crops) the yield per hectare in the years between 1923 and 1927 was 1·067 food units; in 1934 it was 1·418. In the years between 1911 and 1913 Finland produced only 41 per cent of the cereals consumed by her population; for 1934 the figure was 82 per cent. In 1920 the yield of milk was 1,865,000,000 kilograms, in 1935 it was 2,728,000,000.[1]

This increased agricultural productivity was the greatest achievement of Finland under the Republic. It is perhaps encouraging to note that the State played a comparatively small part in promoting it. Though the Government undertook research work, provided loans and subsidized the farmers (as we shall see) in time of crisis, responsibility for the striking progress in agriculture lies not so much with the State as with the individual farmers who, once freed from hopeless conditions of lease and labour, proved them-

---

[1] See *Suomen Tilastollinen Vuosikirja*, the official year-book of statistics (Helsinki, 1936).

selves one of the most progressive groups of producers in the world. The key to their success is to be found in their infinite capacity for taking pains and in their extraordinary collaboration through the co-operative movement.

It is the peculiarity of the northern peoples that they combine a passion for peasant proprietorship with a habit of collaboration. "Since time immemorial common enterprises have been carried on among the Finnish people in all spheres of pure economy in kind. Such common enterprises consisted, for instance, in the sphere of fishing of drag-net crews that have preserved their old form down to our own day along the sea-coast and on the shores of the larger lakes. In the sphere of forestry there were common associations, hunting teams for the purpose of destroying wolves in particular, in the sphere of reindeer-breeding grazing crews, in the sphere of cattle-farming common pastures, in the sphere of agriculture burn-beating companies. In all these associations there was, as in present-day co-operative societies, equal membership and democratic management, they were voluntary and the surplus they yielded was divided according to what each member had contributed as his share in establishing the association."[1] When at the end of the last century the cash and credit system replaced the old subsistence economy, the country folk were lost; they fell a prey to the usurer and the dealer and could think of no way of translating their habit of collaboration into terms of the new economy.

The solution was first proposed by a Professor Palmén who gave a lecture in 1866 on the work of the Rochdale Pioneers. He told how in 1844 twenty-eight Rochdale

[1] Pellervo-Seura (editors), *Agricultural Co-operation in Finland* (Helsinki, 1936).

workmen had collected a pound apiece for the purchase of sacks of flour; the flour was retailed at market prices from the cottage of one of the members in Toad Lane and the profit was divided among the subscribers in proportion to the amount of their purchases. From this beginning a co-operative movement had grown up in England, Germany and Scandinavia. Could not Finns adopt this method of self-help to free themselves from the extortions of the middlemen?

Palmén's lecture fell upon stony ground. It was not until 1899 when Dr. Hannes Gebhard founded a society (called Pellervo, after the old Finnish God of Fertility) for the dissemination of co-operative ideas that the idea really began to take root among the rural population of Finland. A law of 1901 gave statutory recognition to co-operative societies observing the following principles: membership open to anyone who would pay the minimum subscription and observe the rules; control exercised by all members on the basis of a single and equal vote; profit divided among members in proportion to their purchases. From that moment the movement grew steadily. In 1903 there were about 18,000 members of co-operative societies; to-day over half the adult population of Finland are co-operators.

The co-operative principle came to be applied to all manner of purposes. Perhaps the most urgent was the provision of credit through Co-operative Credit Banks. "A bank," wrote the Italian Luigi Luzzati, "is an institution where the money of the poor is lent out to the rich; a Co-operative Credit Bank an institution where the money of the poor is lent out to the poor." The idea was first worked out by one Raiffeisen in South Germany where societies of villagers pooled their scanty savings and pledged their bit of credit to provide loans for the needy. Professor Gebhard developed the Raiffeisen system in Finland. In 1902 he founded the Central Bank for Co-operative Societies (O.K.O.). Without the facilities thus provided the peasant could never have purchased his land, raised his buildings, purchased his tools or improved his stock. At the end of 1935 there were 1,299 little banking societies with a total membership of 140,000, and the credits granted to them by O.K.O. amounted to 1,049,000,000 marks. It is worth noting that the difference between the interest rates paid for deposits and the rates charged for loans was on the average only 1·25 per cent. The difference during the same year in England on the joint-stock banking system was nearly 4 per cent.

Besides credit the farmer had two other vital needs. First he needed help as a producer: he could not hope to own his own bull, his own threshing-machine, his own butter-churn; alone he could not hope to sell his produce in the best market. Secondly he needed help as a consumer: alone he could not hope to buy his sugar, coffee and boots at a fair price; every step he took beyond the old subsistence-economy brought him more under the thumb of the profiteering middleman. Both these needs were met, and amply met, by co-operation.

On the produce side the most important co-operative efforts were devoted to dairy-farming, for half the farm-land is under pasture and fodder crops, and half the farmers' money income comes from milk products. Privately owned dairies on the great estates had mulcted the tenants unmercifully, and the joint-stock dairies which flourished between 1895 and 1902 made profits for every one except the farmer. In 1903 the first co-operative dairies were established with the encouragement of Pellervo. They "are owned by their milk suppliers in common, every member contributing to the costs of erection, maintenance, and business, in precise proportion as he utilizes the services of the creamery, and participating in any trading surplus in exact proportion to his milk supplies."[1] By the end of 1934 there were 684 co-operative dairies with 75,000 members in all. Again the point to note is the low cost of these co-operative services to the farmer: in 1935 he received 84 per cent of the price paid for butter by the consumers.

Besides the dairies all manner of agricultural producers' co-operative societies have grown up—bull societies, moss-litter societies, and lately bacon factories and egg-selling societies. Two great central organizations have been formed, the first, Hankkija, for supplying farmers' equipment, and the second, Valio, for marketing dairy produce abroad. Hankkija supplies co-operative shops and dairies with fertilizer and cattle-food, seed and grain, machinery and electric power-heating installations and refrigerators. It manufactures about 15 per cent of the articles it sells and has been a pioneer in the manufacture of several types of agricultural machinery, notably of the famous Esa thresher. Valio has done equally important work, making itself responsible for the export of dairy produce, which amounts to a fifth of the total exports of the country. Its activities have embraced research and quality control, grading and the manufacture of new products, such as Dutch types of cheese, as well as the business of foreign sales. Nearly 94 per cent of the Finnish exports of butter pass through Valio's hands.

On the consumer side co-operation began among the

[1] Thorsten Odhe, *Finland: A Nation of Co-operators* (1931).

135

industrial workers and it was through their initiative that the first Finnish Co-operative Wholesale Society (SOK) was created in 1904. The business of SOK was primarily to buy and manufacture food, clothing and household utensils for the member-societies which were rapidly springing up in country as well as town areas. It was organized on a democratic basis, each member-society having an equal vote in the affairs of SOK. Here a difficulty arose. The rural societies were usually very much smaller than those in the towns and the latter naturally felt it unfair that their vote should count for no more than that of a parish union with a handful of members and insignificant capital. They were particularly angry when the rural societies refused to accept the principle that only Trade Union members should be employed. A quarrel developed and led to a split in 1916, when a number of urban societies seceded from SOK and in the following year founded a wholesale society of their own (OTK). Henceforward Finnish consumer-co-operation developed through two separate channels. SOK became known as the Neutral Society and drew its strength chiefly from the conservative farming community. OTK was called the Progressive Movement and drew its strength largely from the Social Democratic industrial workers. Yet the distinction was not so clear as might be expected. Both movements were careful not to affiliate themselves with any political party. Neither restricted its appeal to any one class or region. Each retained the same co-operative principles, keeping the minimum subscription demanded from individuals as low as possible—ten shillings is an average figure—and aiming at low prices and increased reserves of capital rather than at high dividends (the dividends in a normal year rarely exceed 2 per cent). Both joined the Scandinavian Wholesale Society in 1928. A healthy rivalry developed between them and their competitive propaganda brought many more members into the co-operative movement than would have been likely under an undivided system. At the same time the division handicapped the movement in two important respects: it split the capital resources and made mass production impossible on the scale which in Sweden was so successful in setting an example in cheapness and efficiency to profit-making companies; and it made consumer co-operation an irritant instead of an emollient in the friction between Haves and Have-nots.

Nevertheless the Finnish consumer-co-operatives have some remarkable achievements to their credit. They set the price-level of a great many articles. The SOK settlement at Vaajakoski and its flour-mills at Viipuri and Oulu are models for the world, and the same may be said for the restaurants of some of the societies affiliated to the Progressive Movement. Of these Elanto, the Helsinki consumers' society, is by far the biggest and the most enterprising. In 1934 it had 48,173 members (of whom 80 per cent were wage-earners), 329 shops including 15 restaurants of varying grades, its turnover amounted to over 288,000,000 marks and its employees numbered 2,400. Elanto sets the standard for all Finland in the manufacture of bread and bacon, in shop and restaurant design and in the treatment of employees. The reputation made by its Social Democratic managing director, Väinö Tanner, raised him to the Prime Ministership in December 1926.

When the history of the Finnish co-operative movement comes to be written, its greatest achievement will no doubt be found in its work as a medium of education. Each of the many central organizations has its own periodical Press. The chief weekly papers of the Neutral and Progressive Societies have a circulation of 182,000 and 130,000 copies respectively among the Finnish-speaking population alone. (An equivalent circulation in Great Britain, where the reading public is about fifteen times as big, would be two-to-three million copies. Which English weekly can boast that?) Each runs its own lecture courses. Every year some 1,400 lectures were delivered to nearly 350,000 listeners under the auspices of KK, the propaganda agency of the Progressive Movement. KK maintains its own staff of architects and has set an example in factory and shop design which older nations might do well to follow. To the co-operative movement the Finnish housewife owes her education in domestic science, the farmer in modern methods of crop- and stock-raising and in book-keeping, the wage-earner in what Quakers used to call the re-creative use of leisure, and the public as a whole in democratic principles and the elements of economics. What the Finnish people would have become without co-operation can never be known; perhaps there would have been no alternative between remaining a poverty-stricken, backward and exploited peasantry or becoming a regimented and collectivized community in the Russian model.

Some idea of the part which co-operation plays in Finland can be gathered from a Swedish writer's[1] account of a journey in Ostrobothnia:

"Still fresh in the author's mind is a visit one frowsy April day to Lapua, where Finland fought one of her bloodiest battles against the Russian invaders in 1809, now a flourishing village in one of the most fertile and best-

[1] Thorsten Odhe, *op. cit.*

cultivated parts of Finland. In the middle of the village stands the stately local authority offices, turreted like a castle, rough-cast, with café and restaurant and other social amenities. Through the village runs the old main road, now a broad highway; along both sides lie the business premises, for the most part co-operative institutions of one kind or another. The parish boasts a population of 14,000, practically all co-operators.

"There are in the parish three consumer co-operative societies, two SOK, one KK, with ten shops amongst them, seven co-operative creameries, six co-operative Credit Banks, a score of bull societies, threshing societies, pig-breeding societies, and, in intimate relation to agricultural co-operative undertakings, eight farmers' guilds, young farmers' clubs, and other mutual improvement associations. Lapuan Osuuskauppa (Co-operative Retail Society), which, with its capacious stores, occupies a substantial brick building in the middle of the village, sells grocery and provisions, drapery and furnishings, boots and shoes, household utensils, feeding stuffs, manures, agricultural machinery and requirements, and markets yearly for its members many thousands of pounds' worth of grain and other produce. Special show-rooms for agricultural machinery, with large display windows, have been built, and at the railway station the society has its own granary with mechanical conveyors, and cleaning and grading machinery. The Society has 1,350 members and an annual turnover of £67,200."

The subjects which aroused the greatest public interest in the early years of the Republic were language, land co-operation and—absurdly enough—Prohibition. For by a bitter irony of history the people who had just won the

139

right to rule themselves dissipated their executive energies on an unenforcable law, and the Republic where so much was being done that deserved the admiration of the Western world became the laughing-stock of Europe (the American eye for humour had a blind spot at this moment) for its attempts to exorcise the alcoholic spirit.

The Prohibition movement was a legacy from the nineteenth century. Every people in every age has taken some form of narcotic drug, and the Finns, whom nature had endowed with neither betel-nut nor tobacco, neither coffee nor tea, neither grapes for wine nor abundant barley for malt, were in the habit of distilling alcohol from wood and corn. But drunkenness did not assume the proportions of a public nuisance until the Industrial Revolution came, bringing with it a need for workers to drown their sorrows in drink and at the same time an opportunity for total immersion. The Russian Government, with an eye on the vodka exports, encouraged the habit. A reaction followed among the Finnish educated classes. The first abstinence society was founded in 1877 and in 1884 the Diet passed a law recognizing the Friends of Temperance and restricting the manufacture and sale of alcohol. Rapidly the movement gathered momentum: in 1899 the Friends of Temperance had 10,000 members and over 70,000 people took the pledge. During the general strike of 1905 the Finnish public had its first taste of Prohibition and seemed to be in no way appalled by it, for in 1907 the reformed Diet passed the first Prohibition Bill in history. But unfortunately the bill made no provision for compensating trade interests or for filling the hole in the revenue which would be left by the cessation of liquor taxes, and the Senate had no difficulty in quashing it —on the unimpeachable ground that it would infringe existing treaties. In 1909 the Diet returned to the attack and passed a second Prohibition Bill. This time it was the Czar who refused to sign it. Kerensky found the bill in the Governmental pigeon-holes and promulgated it in May 1917 with the provision that two years were to elapse before it came into force.

With this mixed parentage Prohibition came to Finland in 1919 on 1 June. Public opinion was more than ever enthusiastic. Not that Finland was a particularly drunken country: on the basis of figures for 1906–10 which showed the consumption of alcohol *per capita* to be one-sixth of that in Great Britain it has been claimed that she was the soberest nation in Europe. But the war years had loosened restraints and drunkenness had fathered a multitude of sins. It came as a shock to the Finnish public to find that the law was not observed; for years they refused to believe that increasing numbers of their community were determined to get drunk at any price. Yet the evidence was obvious to anyone who set foot in a town or cast eyes on a newspaper. Convictions for drunkenness increased from 12,200 in 1910, to 87,191 in 1927, to 101,500 in 1929. The legal consumption of alcohol (for medical purposes!) rose from 1·7 million litres in 1920 to 5·1 million in 1927; and the increase in illegal consumption of course defied measurement. In Finland as in America illicit drinking became the favourite sport of the rich and the ambition of the adolescent.

The Government did what it could. A Committee of Inquiry into the working of the law was set up in 1922, an agreement for checking smuggling was signed with the other states of the Baltic in 1925, an act restricting the right of doctors to prescribe alcoholic medicines was passed in 1928, the budget grant for temperance propaganda and supervision was increased from 190,000 marks in 1919 to 3,545,000 in 1929, and the grant for Police and Customs from 34,000,000 to 134,000,000 marks within the same period.[1] All in vain: the indented, islanded coastlines of Finland seemed given by God for the shelter of smugglers; the new motor transport seemed specially invented to make every car owner a potential publican. An unignorable minority of the nation persisted in defying the Prohibition law, and an unshakable majority persisted in refusing its repeal.

The persistence of the Prohibition movement is not easy to account for. It began as a phase of the religious revivalism that swept Finland in the middle of the nineteenth century: the alcoholic ecstasy is so near to the revivalistic ecstasy that pastors saw their first duty to lie in crusading against it. Then in the first fine careless rapture of democracy when it seemed that legislation could do anything, in Dicey's phrase, except make a man a woman or a woman a man, the Finns naturally thought to abolish vice as well as injustice by act of parliament, and they made Prohibition the test case. But after a few years it became obvious that Prohibition was something other than a religious or a political movement. Like the language controversy, it concealed a class-conflict; like the land controversy, it was a struggle of Haves against Have-nots. Of the political parties, the Social Democrats had put Prohibition on their platform from the first. The Agrarians, too, were consistently in favour of it, and blamed the upper classes, especially the magistrates and provincial governors, for its non-enforcement. The upper-class parties did not dare, in the face of popular opinion, to denounce Prohibition at the outset, but they gave it little

[1] See J. H. Wuorinen, *The Prohibition Experiment in Finland* (New York, 1931).

backing in their Press. The Concentrationists' paper, *Uusi Suomi,* gave Prohibition no support after 1926. *Hufvudstadsbladet,* the Swedish People's Party paper, opposed it from the beginning. Only the Progressive paper, the *Helsingin Sanomat*—incidentally the best daily in Finland—took a rational attitude and proposed a referendum. This was rigorously opposed by all parties except the Progressives— by the Right because they had no hope of a majority and by the Left because representative institutions are invariably weakened by referendums and they had no wish to constitute a dangerous precedent.

Perhaps the Right was right. Perhaps the nation had been betrayed by the culpable idealism of inexperienced politicians of the Left into passing legislation that could not be enforced. Certainly it was human nature rather than a mere conspiracy of vested interests that wrecked the Prohibition experiment. And wherever the blame may lie Finland had learned by the failure a salutary lesson about the limits of the sphere of legislation. She may have learned an equally salutary and more subtle lesson that disobedience to a popular law may itself be popular. Yet when all is said it is surprising that Prohibition was not repealed until 1932 and then only under pressure of the greatest economic crisis in the short history of the Republic.

CHAPTER 8

ECONOMIC CRISIS

AND POLITICAL REACTION

1929–31

"The Finns are extremely wild." TACITUS

HAPPY indeed is the nation that has no history. During the nineteen-twenties the eyes of Europe were turned on the halting progress of Weimar Germany, on Italy in the birth-pangs of Fascism, on the new economic policies and plans of Soviet Russia. These were the countries that were making history in the twenties; the world has no attention for the democracies of the Scandinavian north, least of all for Finland. After the settlement of the Åland dispute almost the only Finnish affair to get into the news was the Prohibition experiment, though there was a word here and there about the not very significant political changes—a note for instance on the minority Social Democratic ministry under Väinö Tanner which took office in 1926. Then suddenly in 1930 Finland sprang into the news. "Fascism in Finland" ran the headlines. Finland was "making history" again.

It all began, absurdly enough, with the announcement of the League of Communist Youth that a propaganda meeting would be held at the end of November 1929 in Lapua. The choice of this village was in itself a provocation. Lapua is not only the centre of the conservative yeoman-farmer community of Ostrobothnia but the site of victories over the Russians in the old days and the first rallying-place of the White forces at the beginning of the civil war. It is also the centre of the Pietists, the sect which above all others had been incensed by the anti-religious propaganda of the Communists.

On the appointed day a train arrived filled with four hundred lads, some of them carrying arms and dressed in red shirts worn outside their trousers in the Russian fashion. The station was crowded, not with the idle and amused crowd which gathers in Finnish country stations to stare at travellers from the distant cities, but with angry farmers who had been encouraged by their pastors to believe that Communism was an insult to God as well as a menace to private property. The lads were attacked, their shirts torn off and their arms seized. A number of them were bundled off in the departing train; the remainder insisted on holding their meeting. The reception they had received did not incline them to mince words, and the farmers had some justification for losing their tempers. They rushed the platform and gave the speakers a good hiding.

There the incident should have ended—with the farmers boasting to their wives over dinner, the pastors looking up texts for anti-Communist sermons, and the local urchins masquerading in the remnants of the red shirts. Instead of which there was a general flare-up. As Professor Lauri Ingman wrote: "A spark had fallen into the tinder at Lapua. And tinder was everywhere in the country. The arrogant behaviour of the Communists had raised feeling to such a pitch in all those circles where the religion and morals handed down by previous generations, love of country, the independence and liberty of the Republic were still held in respect, that in a few days a mighty wave of anti-Communist feeling had spread like a conflagration throughout the country."[1]

On 1 December a mass meeting was held in Lapua. The moving spirit, Vihtori Kosola, a farmer who had been imprisoned in St. Petersburg for separatist activity in the Russian days, set the key at once: "Is it not time to carry into execution that decision of the Supreme Court which orders the suppression of Communist organizations of any description with all their organs? The decision needs no amendment, all that is needed is to carry it into effect." The meeting passed a number of resolutions to this effect and issued a circular to similar gatherings which were held in the next few weeks in various parts of the country: "The mass meeting at Lapua appeals to all sane-thinking citizens in the hope that a united firm front can be created against the agitation and treasonable insolence of the Communists. By co-operation on our side we must help the authorities to smother the propaganda meetings and disgraceful imitations of Bolshevik customs at their birth. A small minority must not be permitted to insult the ideas of a whole nation regarding morals, justice, religion and patriotism. The measure of treasonable Communist audacity is now full. This is keenly felt in Ostrobothnia and surely all over the country. For this reason the disturbances in Lapua are easy to understand. To prevent the recurrence of such events in the near future the will of the people must crush this illegal revolutionary party in all its phases."

Before long deputations from Ostrobothnia, Häme, Satakunta and other provinces were making their way to the capital. President Relander and the Prime Minister, Kyosti

[1] L. Ingman, *The Lapua Anti-Communist Movement* (Helsinki, 1930).

Kallio, received them sympathetically, assuring them that Communist activity would be stopped by every means in the power of the law. The difficulty was that the law as it stood had very little power; by changing its name the Communist party had legally evaded the restrictions imposed in 1923. The Diet was thereupon asked to pass a bill making the suppression of certain Communist societies possible; this it did. Then it was asked to amend the Press laws so that Communist propaganda might be muzzled; this it refused to do. The fifty-nine Socialist members joined the twenty-three Communist members in their determination not to be stampeded by the Lapua movement into ending the freedom of the Press for ever.

The farmers met this by setting up a permanent organization of their own. At a meeting held in Lapua in March 1930 an association called Suomen Lukko (Finland's Lock) was formed to combat Communism. "For the realization of this goal," read the Lukko programme, "public opinion must be educated to a pitch that will result in the clear and definite emergence of a strongly antagonistic tendency in the legislation of this country towards Communist activity." The formation of Suomen Lukko meant that the Lapua movement had turned to direct action. On the night of 27 March, a printing press in Vaasa was smashed to pieces; the reason was that it printed *Työn Ääni* (Labour's Voice). In the months that followed reports came from all over the country that Communists had been abducted, some beaten, some locked up, some taken in cars to the Russian frontier and thrown over the boundary wire. On 4 June the counsel for *Työn Ääni* was seized outside the court and driven over the Swedish frontier. On 5 July two Communist members of the Diet were kidnapped at a meeting

147

of a Standing Committee and taken to Lapua for punishment. Against all this the arm of the law was impotent. The provincial police were unable, even if they had been willing, to protect Communists. Kyösti Kallio, the Prime Minister, bowed before the storm. He ordered the suppression of Communist papers on his own responsibility on 1 July, and on the following day asked the Diet to authorize his action. Then he resigned, and President Relander called into office what in England would be called a National Government—a coalition representing all the propertied parties. None of the actual Lapuan leaders were in the new Cabinet, but seven of the thirteen members were not members of the Diet and the only minister who survived from the Kallio regime was Procopé, the Secretary for Foreign Affairs, a non-party man who was retained to calm opinion abroad. The new Premier was Svinhufvud, the White leader who had been in retirement since 1922 and now was recalled to office at the age of sixty-nine, an elder statesman with the prestige of a *Pater Patriae*.

To bring pressure on the new Government Kosola, who was beginning to see himself as a sort of Finnish Mussolini, staged a March on Helsinki. On 7 July, twelve thousand farmers arrived in the capital and were welcomed by President Relander and General Mannerheim. Their spokesman was Kares, a Pietist pastor of great demagogic power who had long used his pulpit in Lapua as a platform against Communism. "We demand," said Pastor Kares, "vigorously, unconditionally and with no room for compromise, the expulsion of Communism in this country from every public field to that subterranean darkness where crime dwells and which is the field of labour of the criminal authorities. We demand the pitiless suppression of all institutions, no matter what their name, which have been created for the maintenance and spreading of Communism. We demand the due punishment of treason in all its forms, even in its preparatory stages. We demand the prohibition of the mockery of religion and the fear of God, and of the spreading of this blasphemous spirit among children and adolescents. We demand the cessation of petty party calculations in Parliament and the creation of combinations and laws which will constantly ensure the existence of strong and lasting Governments in this country. We demand that the cause of the Fatherland and righteousness be no longer a subject of barter. For ourselves, for our class we demand only that a patriotic workman be allowed to maintain himself and his family in peace by his labours, and that from every place of employment every one who violates this right or insults those who once took part in the liberation of this country be dismissed without mercy. This we demand and will abate nothing of our demand. We are ready to fade again into obscurity, each to his labours, but only on the day we see our demands on the road to real fulfilment and only until we are once more needed."

Under such threats Svinhufvud lost no time in putting his programme before the Diet. First, on 8 July, he had the twenty-three Communist members arrested and on the 9th, secured the approval of the mutilated House for his action. Then he asked for the immediate passage of three bills: the first to "forbid the entrance into Parliament of members of a party working for the overthrow of the State, likewise their right to sit in municipal councils," the second to "restrict the possibilities of a misuse of the freedom of the Press for subversive propaganda," the third to give the Government power to deal with emergencies by ordinance.

Now these bills constituted an amendment of the Constitution: therefore they needed to be passed by a two-thirds majority and to be ratified by a similar majority of a new House after a general election. The alternative was to declare them an emergency measure, in which case a majority of five-sixths would have been needed to pass them immediately. Svinhufvud could have obtained his two-thirds majority now that the Communist members were expelled, but he did not want to risk a general election in the country's present inflamed mood. He tried to carry them under emergency regulations, but the Social Democrats, who were unwilling to accept them in unamended form, blocked the five-sixths majority. There was nothing for it but to face an election. Svinhufvud dissolved the Diet on 15 July, and announced that a general election would be held at the beginning of October.

The situation was now dangerous. The Minister of the Interior announced on 18 July: "under no circumstances will treasonous activity disguised as political campaigning be tolerated. Therefore, the election meetings or other similar election activity on the part of the Communists must be prevented by the police." The Social Democrats wanted a third of the seats in the new Diet; if they could get them the new laws could not go through. And there was every probability that they would get them, for the votes which had elected twenty-three Communists in 1929 would presumably be cast for Social Democrats now that the Communist party was proscribed. In that case there was every probability of civil war, for the Lapuans did not attempt to conceal their intention to fight if the laws were not passed. Meanwhile they resorted to the most illegal forms of electioneering. They formed no separate political party but gave their support to all right-wing organizations and terrorized local authorities into erasing the names of Communists from the lists of electors. They kidnapped the leader of the Social Democratic Party, Väinö Hakkila, took him to a deserted place in the north and threatened him with death. Throughout August and September there were abductions of Socialists as well as Communists. And the Government connived at these excesses; as Svinhufvud admitted afterwards: "political unrest had been so intense that strong measures by the Government would have resulted in bloodshed and civil war, as the Lapuans were determined to accomplish their objects."

It must have appeared to all outside observers that Finland had gone stark, staring mad. In one short year the cardinal principles on which the Republic had been founded were thrown aside like yesterday's newspaper. Gone was the much-vaunted respect for law; the very classes which had been legality's greatest champions were the first to encourage terrorism. Gone was the belief in individual liberties; clergymen preached intolerence as a Christian duty, democrats urged the disenfranchisement of a large proportion of their fellow citizens, the farmers—individualists to a man—conspired to end the right of free speech and public meeting. Gone was the level-headedness, the "canniness" that had been acclaimed as a national characteristic; half the nation was ranting against the Communists for all the world as if they were incarnations of the Devil or had intended another insurrection on the lines of January 1918. It was the suddenness of the movement that was most surprising. After all, the Communists, like the poor, they had always with them. Every one had accepted the continued existence of the party since by a change of name it had evaded the law of 1923. Every one had known that they were increasing their hold on the Trade Unions. Their numbers had been growing—twenty Communist seats in the Diet in 1927 were increased to twenty-three in 1929—but there was little in that to terrify men of property. Their relations with Moscow were intimate but there was nothing to show that Moscow was arming them for revolt. Their behaviour had been insolent, but it had also been futile. They had announced a general strike for 16 November, 1929, to obtain the release of some of their members who were awaiting trial for treasonable activities, but when the day came the workers took no notice of the strike proclamation and factories and shops worked normal hours. What, then, had come over the impassive and cautious Finn? What was the explanation of the extraordinary movement that came to birth in Lapua?

The explanation lies in the economic structure of Finland and in the shock it sustained in the years 1928–30.

Finland entered on the post-war period with two great natural assets—her land and her forests—and with two great unnatural liabilities—the heavy debts contracted in the war years and the loss of her best customer, Russia. The first liability was minimized by inflation and by Risto Ryti's stabilization of the mark in 1924 at one-sixth of its former value; thus industrialists and farmers were able to pay off their debts on the easiest terms and exporters were given a favourable opportunity to penetrate new markets. The assets were increased, the first as we have seen by the Government's land reforms and by the co-operative organization of agriculture; the second by the application of new machinery and electric power to wood-working, and by the increased demand, especially from Great Britain, for timber, sawn wood, pulp, paper, plywood, cellulose and other wood products. So for Finland as for the world in general the period between 1922 and 1928 was one of extraordinary economic expansion.

The mainspring of the boom is to be found in the export of wood products. Prices remained high and the volume of trade increased: between 1922 and 1927 the amount of timber cut for export purposes increased by 63 per cent. The effects of this were felt by every class of the community. Exporters realized big profits and extended their plant, agricultural workers found plentiful winter employment in the timber camps. There was more money available for consumption purposes, and consequently imports of food-stuffs—particularly cereals, sugar and coffee—increased and new home industries were set up to cater for the demand for manufactured goods and for housing accommodation. The building trade enjoyed the greatest expansion—the towns of Finland were practically rebuilt during this period. Altogether the number of industrial workers increased by 19·8 per cent and the capacity of the home industries by 40·7 per cent.

The first sign that the boom was nearing its peak came early in 1928. As might be expected the danger signal was given by the wood industry. The four great timber-exporting countries of Europe—Finland, Sweden, Poland and Russia—had increased their output by 25 per cent between 1926 and 1927: obviously this was more than the market could bear without a serious fall in prices, and from such a fall Finland had most to lose, for wood products consti-tuted 83 per cent of her total exports while they were but 55 per cent of Sweden's. In May 1928 the Finnish Sawmill Association agreed to restrict production by 10 per cent.

The second danger signal took the form of a financial crisis. The boom had been accompanied by a shortage of capital: the savings of the Finnish people were not nearly enough for all the borrowers needing loans to finance increased production. The Government tried to meet the need by investing 220,000,000 marks in the current accounts of commercial banks in March 1928, but in August this money was needed for other purposes and the loan was withdrawn. Producers now found themselves in sore straits for capital. Farmers who relied on short-term loans had to pay more for their advances, much more than many of them could afford, as is shown by the number of public auctions of real estate which increased five-fold between 1927 and 1929. Industrialists turned to foreign loans, especially in the building industry where large sums were raised abroad to complete contracts for residential buildings. By the end of 1929 Finland was faced with an unfavourable trade balance of 1,760,000,000 marks, a startling figure compared with the deficit for 1928 which had been only 62,000,000. "The past year," admitted the *Finland Bank Review* in its Bulletin of January 1930, "was in some respects the worst that the economic life of Finland has had to endure for a long time."

If the year 1929 was bad, 1930 was worse. The total value of foreign trade declined, in comparison with the 1928 figure, by 6 per cent in 1929 and by 25 per cent in 1930. The State revenue was 27,000,000 marks lower in 1930 than in 1929, and the fall would have been much more severe had it not been for raised customs duties. Reduced profits meant reduced output and reduced output meant less employment. The extent of the unemployment cannot be accurately measured because there are no figures for Finland as a whole: only 217 out of some 600 communes supported employment boards and the only available figures are those which the boards supply. According to these there were 886 registered unemployed in September 1928, 2,465 in September 1929, 6,220 in September 1930 and 11,754 at the lowest depths of the depression in January 1931. Perhaps we should multiply by four to get an idea of the total unemployed. Even this may not seem serious in a country of 3,600,000 people, but it must be remembered that this was Finland's first taste of serious unemployment; the worst she had known before was a thousand or two workless men in the winter months, and there was no provision made by the State for unemployment insurance.

Such was the economic background in which the seeds of the Lapua movement germinated. Similar movements of political reaction were to arise in every capitalist country in the face of the economic crisis: in England the Labour Government fell in 1931, in France the Republic was endangered by the riots of February 1932, in Germany the Weimar Republic succumbed to Hitlerism in January 1933. In each the symptoms were, *mutatis mutandis*, the same: falling prices led to loss of profits, loss of trade, unemployment, trade barriers, increased taxation and an attempt to reduce the wages and allowances of the working-class. Dislocation was naturally greatest in countries like America where the slump came most suddenly: Finland was fortunate in having a private crisis of her own in 1928 before the general crisis set in. This is no place for an analysis of the causes underlying the fall in prices and the world economic crisis in general, but in order to understand the Finnish crisis in particular attention must be drawn to three factors which were peculiar to that country.

In the first place the initial impact of the slump hit the smallholders more severely than any other class of the community. They suffered in 1928 through the failure of the harvest as well as through the rise of interest-rates on short-term loans. In 1929 they suffered again from the scarcity of employment in the lumber camps on which so many of them depended for their living in the hard winter months. The Finnish unemployment figures include a unique category labelled "Landowners"; there were 7,900 landowners registered as unemployed in December 1930.[1] The industrial workers of the towns did not feel the slump until later; in the building industry, for instance, unemployment did not become severe until 1931. And the workers who were in employment continued to benefit by the fall in retail prices; it is noteworthy that League of Nations statistics show the cost of living to have fallen more in Finland between 1928 and 1930 than in any other European country except Estonia. The small farmers, then, might reasonably feel that they had a grievance, and it was among the small farmers that the Lapua movement began.

Secondly the potential danger of Communist Russia was felt more acutely in Finland than in any other country. The agriculturists had been deprived of their winter employment by the decreased output of the timber trade, and to them the timber crisis could admit of only one explanation: Russia was dumping large quantities of timber abroad at a price far below the cost of production. Dr. Suviranta in a survey made for the Finnish Economic Council[2] quoted the Moscow correspondent of the *New York Times* as saying that on 2 February, 1929, there were about 1,000,000

[1] See *Suomen Tilastollin Vuosikirja*.
[2] Bv. Suviranta, *Finland and the World Depression* (Helsinki, 1931).

political exiles in Russia, of whom perhaps 200,000 were in northern timber camps; he further quoted Professor Haensel's calculation that the Soviet Government had devoted as premiums for aiding unprofitable export the sum of 68,000,000 roubles in the budget of 1927–28 and 114,000,000 roubles in the budget of 1928–29; and he concluded: "Thus the Russian export trade is based upon the exploitation of natural resources and human power, artificial prices, export premiums, and trade monopoly. In these circumstances any prices prevailing on foreign markets may be deliberately undercut. The low export prices thus created represent, of course, a gift to the purchasers, as is always the case with dumping, and an economic loss to the seller. But this is only one and the less important aspect of the question. Of much more weight is the resulting confusion in world markets, where calculations based upon rational economics and ordinary business methods are thereby nullified. In this way the Russian dumping necessarily inflicts serious economic damage on other countries. And with the world already suffering from general depression, such a dumping policy, unchecked, is bound to have disastrous effects upon the possibilities of trade recovery. This certainly was the case in 1930." If a financial expert can write like this of the contributory influence of Russian policy on the crisis it is easy to imagine how simple farmers came to see it as the sole cause. They had all been brought up in veneration of their ancestors who had fought against Russia in 1809, some of them, like Kosola, had seen the inside of Russian prisons, most of them had fought against Bolshevik-aided Reds in 1918. To all of them Russia, whether Czarist or Marxist, was the eternal enemy. To all of them Communism connoted the loss of their land and their freedom. If the Soviet Union were to undertake a policy of expansion, the first victim would be Finland. There is little wonder that the Finnish farmers saw Russian machinations behind their economic crisis and turned on the Communists in their midst who were at one with Russia in ideals if not already in allegiance.

The third factor which determined the peculiar nature of the Lapua movement was the part played by the Lutheran clergy. In every peasant country, with the exception of Soviet Russia, the clergy are powerful, and circumstances had made them particularly powerful in Finland. There was no squire in the villages to share their moral authority; there was no dissenting movement to fill nonconformist chapels at the expense of the parish churches, for the Pietism that swept the country districts a century ago was kept within the pale of Lutheran orthodoxy. Until the middle of the nineteenth century the pastors were schoolmasters as well as priests, for no one could be confirmed until he had learned to read and there was no one except the pastor to teach him. Under the Republic 98 per cent of the population were listed as Lutherans and every one, whether Lutheran or not, was obliged to pay taxes for the upkeep of the State Church. One acre in every hundred of forest and nearly one acre in every hundred of cultivated land belonged to the Church. The Church had kept its authority, as it had kept its property, in the country districts, but there was no doubt that the drift to the towns meant a drift away from religion. Always when it feels its religious hold slipping a Church turns to political action, and to this the Finnish hierarchy was no exception. The clergy threw themselves into the Nationalist movement, they produced spokesmen on both the Finnish and the Swedish side in the language controversy, they organized the Prohibition movement and they supplied the most unforgiving among the White leaders in the civil war. Then, in the post-war years, they made themselves the champions of the faithful against Communism. The more real the Communist menace, the greater the need for the bulwark of the Church; the clergy would not have been human if they had not exaggerated the danger from Russia, had not insisted on the complicity of the Finnish Communists with Moscow and professed to see little difference between Communists and Social Democrats. In a sense they were right: Socialism in whatever form is essentially utilitarian; its victory would mean a defeat for organized religion. But in a sense they were wrong: the defeat of organized religion would not necessarily involve the overthrow of national independence, social justice and conventional morality. The pastors were responsible for making these defeats appear as inseparable consequences of Socialism in the eyes of the Finnish masses. Thanks to the efforts of Kares, Danielson, Arvi Järventaus and a hundred other pastors, Lapua became a religious movement with all the blindness, intolerance and intransigence that consciousness of a supernatural sanction implies.

That the movement should have seemed religious to its supporters is not surprising; every considerable political movement must have an element of religion in its conception. But it is surprising that the preachers of violence in post-war Finland were also ministers of an established Christian faith. Nineteenth-century nonconformity in Great Britain and the United States took a humanitarian form; in Finland it was made of sterner stuff. The Pietists stressed the severity of man's long fight against sin; arming themselves with the weapons of asceticism they mortified their own flesh and thought little of mortifying the flesh of the faith-less. They are more like the Puritans of the seventeenth century than nonconformists of the nineteenth; Oliver Cromwell rather than John Bright is their prototype. Perhaps it was only to be expected that in among the regulation black clothes of the Pietist was the black shirt of the Fascist.

When at last October came the general election passed off quietly. The Social Democrats won 66 seats out of the 200 in the new Diet. If they had won 67 they could have commanded the one-third minority necessary to block the Lapua legislation. As it was the anti-communist bills went through on 11 November by the narrowest possible margin —134 votes to 66.

So far the Lapuan movement had been supported by the majority of the Finnish people, but now that Communism was outlawed and the ostensible aims of the movement attained the masses withdrew their support. Public opinion was behind Svinhufvud's attempt to restore law and order; four hundred men surrendered themselves voluntarily to the courts for trial for complicity in terrorist activities. But the Lapuan movement did not die. Shorn of popular support it stood out for what it essentially was: a conspiracy of certain capitalist interests to establish a form of Fascist dictatorship in Finland. It was financed by the Neutral Co-operative Movement which hoped to crush the Progressives, and by the timber exporters who hoped to reduce timbermen's wages. Private banks are said to have paid 15,000,000 marks into the funds of the movement. The chiefs of the army had been implicated in Suomen Lukko and had alarmed the Soviet Government by their liaison with

Polish military authorities. There were forces in the country which were by no means content to return to a regime of parliamentary democracy even now that the Communist snake was scotched.

The habit of terrorism died hard. After the October elections a group of terrorists led by General Kurt Wallenius kidnapped ex-President Ståhlberg and his wife. What they expected to gain by that is difficult to see, for Ståhlberg was widely popular, and it was known that he would stand for re-election in the Presidential elections which were due to take place in January 1931. A general outcry was followed by the release of Ståhlberg, but Kosola's paper *Aktivisti* continued to hint at assassination in the event of his being elected. The January polls proved the popularity of Ståhlberg by returning a record vote for his party, the Progressives. In the electoral college Social Democrats and Progressives combined in support of Ståhlberg while Concentrationists, Swedes and Agrarians voted for Svinhufvud. The latter was elected by 151 votes to 149. Like the anti-Communist legislation, the Presidential election was won by the Right by the margin of one single vote.

Not content with the elevation of Svinhufvud to the Presidency the Lapuan "activists" continued their policy of terrorism. Throughout 1931 kidnappings of Socialists and of over-inquisitive journalists continued. In July General Wallenius was acquitted of complicity in the Ståhlberg outrage, a decision which, as J. H. Wuorinen remarked, "occasioned extensive comment in the press of the country, largely because General Wallenius had made a full confession of his guilt at the time when charges were first preferred against him."[1]

[1] In *Current History* (New York), August 1931.

The prospect was black for Finland. Everything depended on the course of the economic slump. Nothing that Finland could do would improve the world economic situation; almost any complication in the general crisis would have its repercussions in Finland. At first the effects of the crisis had not been unmitigatedly bad. The financial collapse on Wall Street in 1929 had enabled Finns to raise the foreign loans they so badly needed upon comparatively easy terms. The fall in world prices had affected Finland's imports more than her exports: "with the same amount of exports she was able to purchase in 1930 nearly 17 per cent more goods than in 1928." But as time went on more and more obstacles were put in the way of foreign trade and in September 1931 a blow came to Finland from an unexpected quarter. On the 21st of the month the British Government empowered the Bank of England to suspend gold payments. Now Great Britain was Finland's best customer: a fall in the value of the pound sterling would mean a fall in the value of Finland's exports. It would also mean a shortage of foreign currency in Finland and therefore an inability to pay for imports from abroad. A week later the Scandinavian countries followed the British example and went off the gold standard. The loss of British was thus followed by a loss of Swedish trade, the shortage of pounds by a shortage of krone. Finland had no alternative but to follow Great Britain and the Scandinavian countries: on 19 October the Diet confirmed the suspension of the gold standard.

By going off gold Finland saved her trade with Great Britain and Scandinavia and the internal value of the mark was not upset, for wholesale prices rose but slightly (from 79 to 82 in October 1931). But she was placed in an unfavourable position *vis-à-vis* the nations which retained the gold standard, for the mark fell by about 25 per cent in relation to gold. Trade generally was hampered by the prevailing uncertainty and home producers in particular were hampered by the depreciation of the currency, having to pay more for their purchases in relation to what they received. Unemployment figures continued to rise. Altogether 1931 was the worst year Finland had known.

The Government could do little but offer palliatives and distractions. The most successful of the latter was its consent to the holding of a referendum on the retention or abolition of Prohibition. In December the public flocked to the polls: over 70 per cent voted for abolition, less than 28 per cent voted for retention. In February 1932 a law was approved which put an end to the twelve years of ill-fated experiment in Prohibition. The liquor trade was put in the hands of a Public Utility Company, a monopoly which brought much-needed revenue into the coffers of the State. As for palliatives, the Government tackled the unemployment problem by a policy of public works. The principle adopted was that the communes were primarily responsible for relief works. The State provided free transport for the unemployed to their place of domicile. To the communes the State offered to pay up to half the wage-bill of relief works and half the expenses of training courses for workers under the age of twenty. The Government further undertook relief works of its own, offering wages up to 80 per cent of the normal wages for each particular job. In these ways between fifty and sixty thousand workers were employed in the winter of 1931–32, chiefly on roads and railways, canals, harbours and land reclamation. The least possible deviation was made from orthodox capitalist principles. "The basic idea," wrote an official spokesman in the *Finland Bank Bulletin*, "is that unemployment will not be cured until enterprise forsakes the paths which it has been accustomed to follow, but which are now unprofitable, for new paths. For a change of this description economic pressure is needed, and it is essential that the pressure represented by unemployment should be allowed to act. Nevertheless, this pressure must be kept within bounds."

For producers the palliatives offered were more merciful. Measures were taken to check the fall in agricultural prices by imposing increased duties on foreign cereals, pork and eggs, and an attempt was made to stimulate demand for the home farmers' produce by making it compulsory for millers to mix home-grown with foreign rye. Furthermore, farmers were allowed some relief in taxation and were offered State facilities for credits.

By such means the bourgeois-coalition Government endeavoured to soften the impact of the slump. Public opinion as a whole was not dissatisfied by its efforts, but the seeds sown by the Lapua movement had produced a crop of dragon's teeth and at any moment insurrection might break out. It was to be a race with time: would the world economic situation improve in time to save Finland from the Fascist "Terror" which must be the inevitable consequence of continued distress and distrust?

CHAPTER 9

RECOVERY AND REORIENTATION

1932-37

"Might of earth will never fail us,
Never while the earth existeth,
When the Givers are propitious
And Creation's daughters aid us."

KALEVALA I, 18

THE year 1932 opened alarmingly. It was rumoured that
Kurt Wallenius, now secretary-general of the Lapua
movement, was planning an armed rising with certain
leaders of the Civic Guard. This body was a survival of the
White Guard of 1918 which had been given legal recognition and a State subsidy under the Republic, on the understanding that it would act as a territorial militia to guard
the country against foreign invasion and Communist
conspiracy. Its numbers had grown to no less than 100,000
men and its officers were in close touch with those of the
regular army, in which Wallenius had until recently been
Chief-of-Staff. There was no question of a Communist
conspiracy in 1932, but some sections of the Guard were
irritated by the leniency shown towards Communists by
von Born, the Minister of Interior, and General Jalander,
the Governor of the Nyland province. This leniency was
to be the excuse for a *coup d'état* which Wallenius was
planning for the middle of March.

The preparation of a secret *coup* involved more intricate organization than Wallenius was capable of: his plans were upset by a premature rising which broke out in the last week of February.

A Socialist speaker had announced a lecture to be held in a hall in Mäntsälä. When the doors opened the hall was rushed by two or three hundred armed men. The usual police protection had been provided for the speaker, but the police had no fire-arms and were powerless against the rioters who dispersed the meeting and then retired in a body and sent an ultimatum to the President demanding the immediate resignation of the entire Cabinet.

The Lapua leaders were not prepared for this, but they supported the ultimatum. Wallenius and Kosola hurried to Mäntsälä and on their orders bodies of armed men began to concentrate at points within march of the capital. They made every attempt to raise the nation against the Government and for a few days it seemed that they might succeed, but the Press came out with a single voice in condemnation of the rising and the situation was saved by a broadcast talk by President Svinhufvud. This veteran Nationalist, very widely revered as the hero of the White campaign of 1918, appealed to the Civic Guards to remember their oath to the Constitution, and explained to them that they were being hoodwinked by a band of extremists who had no following in the nation into taking illegal action to supplant a popularly elected Government. Svinhufvud's voice turned the scale; the rebel camps broke up and some six thousand insurgents surrendered their arms and slipped away to their homes. Only three or four hundred stood fast round Wallenius at Mäntsälä. They were surrounded by loyalist troops and eventually they too saw that the game was up and dispersed quietly. The rising, which had lasted for seven days, ended without a shot fired on either side.[1]

The democratic Republic had had a narrow escape, and the Government hastened to remove the less unreasonable of the insurgents' grievances. General Jalander's resignation was accepted. A haul of twenty Communists was made early in April and eleven of them were sentenced to imprisonment with hard labour. To the Mäntsälä rebels the Minister of Justice showed remarkable leniency. It was 26 July before the 116 prisoners were brought to trial and then only 52 were sentenced, and the sentences in no case amounted to more than thirty months' imprisonment. Kosola and Wallenius, who seems to have had a charmed life, were merely bound over for three years.

There is an obvious difference between the Lapua movement of 1932 and the movement of 1930. In the beginning Lapua had the support of the propertied classes as a whole, in 1932 it had lost that support. The reason for the change was partly the irresponsible conduct of the Lapuan leaders and partly the improvement in the economic situation. There were signs in 1932 that the worst trough of the depression had passed. Exports were increasing for the first time since 1928; imports also were beginning to rise. The saw-milling industry was optimistic and the textile and metal industries had ceased to complain. The agriculturalists were still in serious difficulties but they had hopes of further Government assistance; the Diet passed a bill for the compulsory lowering of interest rates and the Cabinet resigned when the President, in December, refused his signature. The brunt of the depression was being borne

[1] See the article by T. M. Kivimäki in the *Finland Trade Review*, March 1932.

by the workers: wages were lower than ever. The propertied classes were beginning to realize that they were in a good position; it was in their interest now to work for law and order and to support any Government that could keep the peace while the forces of economic recovery were gathering momentum.

Deprived of the support of public opinion, the Lapua movement fell to pieces. These pieces showed a diversity which was equalled only by their absurdity. With the triennial elections in view—they were due to take place in July 1933—a Military Force party entered the lists, whose leader Captain Kalsta was not ashamed to admit direct inspiration from Hitler. Canvassing was also undertaken by an authoritarian Peasants party which had had its birth in a dispute with the authorities of the parish of Nivala over a decrepit horse. In the remains of the official Lapua party a racial cleavage appeared. In the movement which in its early days had united Finnish- and Swedish-speaking Finns in the common cause of capitalist dictatorship, the Swedo-Finns were now condemned as gradualists. The Lapua leaders changed the name of their party to the Popular Patriotic Movement, known by the initial letters of its Finnish title, IKL. Its uniform was banned and the only distinguishing marks it retained were the black shirt of the Pietists and the blue and black colours displayed on badges, emblems and stationery. The programme of the IKL was nebulous, amounting to little but an insistence on the abolition of the party system, on the outlawing of Social Democracy along with every form of Marxism, and on the granting of plenary powers to the executive for the extinction of every minority except themselves.

It was not expected that these orts of Fascism would have

much appeal to the electorate, but it was widely held that the older right-wing parties would win a victory at the elections. "The signs point to a strengthening of the political Right," wrote the *Finland Trade Review* for June, "whether slight or appreciable remains to be seen." For once the augurs misread the omens: the elections of July 1933 showed a loss of twelve seats by the Concentrationists and a gain of twelve by the Social Democrats. The IKL won only fourteen seats. Except for this new Fascist party the composition of the new Diet was almost the same as that of 1927; Finland was returning to its political balance of pre-crisis days.

The task of restoring the economic balance was not to be so easy. True, international trade was improving—imports and exports were maintaining the upward trend which they had showed in 1932, and now the level of real wages was beginning to rise; but it was not to be expected that the return to normal conditions would take place spontaneously. It was all very well for the Governor of the Bank of Finland to boast of the Government's adherence to *laisser-faire*: "So far Finland has not, on her own initiative," he declared, "taken part in the international race for the destroyal [*sic*] of world trade and towards general impoverishment. On the contrary we have been one of the few countries which have not resorted to restrictions of an exceptional character on imports, and which have placed no check on payments for imports. We have not even restricted the free movement of capital; everyone in this country has been at liberty to take and invest his capital wherever he liked. We have also conscientiously effected all foreign payments up to the present. In fact, we are one of the only debtor countries in the world that has been able to maintain such an attitude."[1] Finland might have weathered the storm without furling her *laisser-faire* sails but she could not hope to make much headway under the old rig. As Risto Ryti pointed out in the course of the same speech: "Finland is dependent on foreign trade to a greater extent than most other countries. We find indeed that during the past few years about one-third of our total production has been sold abroad. Amongst European countries only Switzerland and Denmark compete with us in this respect." It was essential, therefore, to find a way of steering Finnish trade into the closed international markets of 1933. *Laisser-faire* was not enough; there must be some degree of State control.

The key to recovery lay in trade with Great Britain. About 47 per cent of Finland's exports went to the United Kingdom in 1932, the second-best customer being the United States which took only 9 per cent. The task of the Finnish Government was therefore to find a way of guaranteeing the continuance of this trade in the face of competition from Britain's imperial customers and her Scandinavian neighbours. There was not a moment to lose, for Great Britain had already entered into trade agreements with the Dominions (at Ottawa) and with Denmark, Norway and Sweden. Finland must undertake to buy more from Great Britain in return for the produce Britain bought from her. She had not much to bargain with—Finland would always need Britain's custom more than Britain would need hers—but she had something: British exporters were not in a mood to ignore even the smallest market in 1933.

At the beginning of September a British Week was celebrated in Helsinki. There, amid the speeches of diplomats and politicians, the banqueting of salesmen and

[1] Quoted in the *Bank of Finland Bulletin*, September 1933.

financiers, the bandying of compliments and platitudes, the ground was cleared for a new exchange of goods between the two countries. The rules of the game were laid down by a trade agreement, signed at the end of the month. The gist of it was that the best-favoured nation treaty of 1923 was confirmed; in addition Britain gave concessions in duties on Finnish birch-wood, ply-wood and bobbins in return for a wide range of Finnish tariff concessions. Finland undertook to buy at least 75 per cent of her coal imports from Great Britain. Considering that only 47 per cent of her coal came from Great Britain in 1930 this would mean a considerable advantage for the United Kingdom. But the advantages were by no means all on one side. Finland kept her markets in the United Kingdom at a time when London politicians and buyers were being beset by her Scandinavian and British Imperial rivals for preferential treatment. The value of Finland's exports to Great Britain rose year by year after the agreement and their percentage of her total exports remained in the neighbourhood of 47 to 50 per cent. On the other hand her imports from the United Kingdom rose by leaps and bounds after the British Week. From 12 per cent of her total exports in 1931 they rose to 19·4 in 1936, in which year she was taking half her imported textiles and a fourth of her imported machinery as well as three-quarters of her coal from Great Britain.[1]

The improvement in trade relations with Great Britain was accompanied by a rift in relations with Germany. Instead of *laisser-faire* Finland had adopted a policy of reciprocity: she would buy from those who bought from her. The Reich refused to buy from her. Germany had

[1] See Keith Jopson, *Economic Conditions in Finland*, 1936 (Department of Overseas Trade, No. 635).

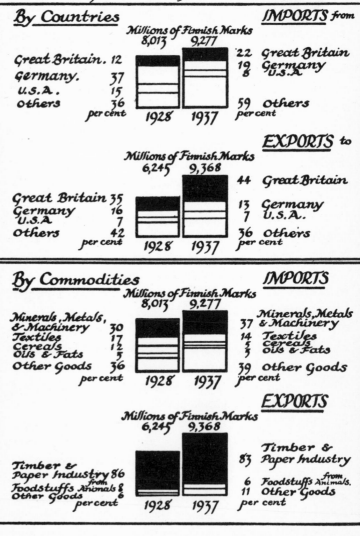

FOREIGN TRADE
in percentages of Total Values

By Countries — IMPORTS from

Millions of Finnish Marks
8,013   9,277

Great Britain. 12
Germany. 37
U.S.A. 15
others 36 per cent

1928   1937

22 Great Britain
19 Germany
8 U.S.A.
59 Others per cent

EXPORTS to

Millions of Finnish Marks
6,245   9,368

Great Britain 35
Germany 16
U.S.A. 7
Others 42 per cent

1928   1937

44 Great Britain
13 Germany
7 U.S.A.
36 Others per cent

By Commodities — IMPORTS

Millions of Finnish Marks
8,013   9,277

Minerals, Metals, & Machinery 30
Textiles 17
Cereals 12
Oils & Fats 5
Other Goods 36 per cent

1928   1937

37 Minerals, Metals & Machinery
14 Textiles
5 Cereals
5 Oils & Fats
39 Other Goods per cent

EXPORTS

Millions of Finnish Marks
6,245   9,368

Timber & Paper Industry 86
Foodstuffs from Animals 8
Other Goods 6 per cent

1928   1937

83 Timber & Paper Industry
6 Foodstuffs from Animals.
11 Other Goods per cent

always exported to Finland very much more than she had imported, and now Hitler was imposing all manner of financial and fiscal restrictions with a view to taking less and less from Finland. The Helsinki Government retaliated by putting a ban on certain German goods. In January 1934 the Finno-German trade agreement, which dated from 1926, was cancelled and a crisis set in which amounted to economic warfare. Not till the end of March was a new agreement signed, and this was not successful in restoring the old trade between the two countries. For instance, Finland did not concede to Germany the preferential duties on textiles which she had granted to Great Britain, and Germany insisted on exchange restrictions which made it impossible for Finnish exporters to get immediate payment for their goods. Germany's share in Finnish imports dropped from 37 per cent in 1928 to 16 per cent in 1936. Her share in Finland's exports did not drop so heavily (from 15·8 per cent to 9·8 per cent in the same period), but the Finns did not receive payment for all of them—50,000,000 Finnish marks remained frozen in the Reichsbank at the end of 1935.

The effect of these changes in commercial relations extended much farther than trade. Throughout the previous century the model to which civilized Finns had looked was German culture. While they took a third of their imports from Germany, they took nearly a third of their ideas. Snellman drew his inspiration from Hegel, Gebhardt from Raffeissen. The first Finnish secondary schools were modelled on the German Lyceums and the first programme of the Finnish Social Democratic Party on the Erfurt programme of the German Socialists. Svinhufvud went to Berlin in search of help against the Reds, and from Weimar were derived many of the conceptions which are embodied in the Finnish Constitution. Helsinki's first public buildings were the work of a German architect, Engel, and the best of the Finnish graduates went to German universities to complete their studies. Western civilization, to the Finn, was in a sense synonymous with German civilization.

This cultural liaison was weakened by the rise of Hitler and by the trade restrictions. English ideas took the place once held by German. Finns wearing English clothes and operating English machines, Finns dealing with English salesmen and working with English technicians could hardly remain immune to the spirit of the country that had sent them. A Finnish-British Society flourished in Helsinki and a similar society sprang to life in Turku in the winter of 1937–38; at both, lecturers sent by the British Council for Foreign Relations found packed and enthusiastic audiences. The London Correspondent of the *Helsingin Sanomat* noted that "there is an unmistakable desire among the younger generation in Finland to look to Great Britain rather than to Germany for cultural ideals. The current of civilization is at last following the trend of trade. Twenty years ago very few Finns visited England, to-day the waitresses in the tourist hotels on the Arctic Coast speak English. The change is, indeed, remarkable. Again, the chief Finnish newspapers now have their own correspondents in London and the Finnish Press generally depends to-day for most of its news on British sources, whereas only a few years ago Berlin was the clearing house for Finland's news of the world."[1]

Though German is still taught as the second language in secondary schools, a school was founded in 1938 at Kapyla outside Helsinki to specialize in the teaching of English. At present we are only at the beginning of the cultural

[1] *The Times*, Trade and Engineering Supplement, June 1936.

rapprochement between Finland and Great Britain; its effects on the former are bound to be enormous, and on the latter they may prove to be not altogether insignificant.

Finland's trend away from Germany is clearly reflected in the sphere of foreign politics. The great bogey in the eyes of the majority of Finns was Soviet Russia: any alliance that would strengthen her against possible aggression by the Soviets was to be welcomed. This feeling found expression in the close contact between Finnish army leaders and the Heimwehr, on one hand, and the pro-German Foreign Minister of Poland, Colonel Beck, on the other. Old General Goemboes of Hungary used to talk of a Central European Bloc which would include Germany, Italy, Austria, Hungary, Poland and—Finland. But with the failure of Wallenius's coups, the unmasking of revolutionary Nazi propagandists in Finland and the difficulties over Finno-German trade, the feeling began to grow that Germany was potentially an enemy rather than an ally. Economic motives urged Finland towards a closer connection with the states whose policy was still to foster international trade rather than to encourage national self-sufficiency.

It happened that a loose agreement between six such states already existed. In December 1930, under pressure of the world crisis, Norway, Sweden, Denmark, Holland, Belgium and Luxemburg had signed what came to be known as the Oslo Convention. They agreed to "apply those principles which underlie the activities of the League of Nations in the economic field," and declared themselves "prepared to support international co-operation which aims at reducing the barriers of trade and to arrive at a general improvement in the conditions for economic relations between countries." In practice this amounted to little but

175

an undertaking to inform each other of proposed changes in customs tariffs and to receive suggestions for modifications in these tariffs. Any hope that the Oslo Group may have entertained of leading the world back to the paths of free trade was shattered by Great Britain's abandoning the gold standard and by her new policy of trade restrictions and imperial preference. Yet the Oslo Group held together and in the autumn of 1931 it was joined by Finland. There was no question of forming an exclusive trade unit: the Oslo Powers comprised a population, including colonials, of 34,000,000, but their trade with each other was insignificant compared with their trade with other nations. They had no illusions about the return of a golden age of commerce: "The Oslo States must accept the fact that the United Kingdom is now a protectionist country and realize clearly that any change in this state of affairs cannot be expected for the rest of this century"—so wrote the Swedish Postmaster-General in June 1937. But they hoped to give a lead, to the United Kingdom and the United States especially, in the direction of "collective action by the large trading countries for easier international trade." The Oslo States, the United Kingdom and the U.S.A. account between them for a third of all world trade.

Political motives combined with economic to urge Finland towards a *rapprochement* with states whose principles were democratic rather than authoritarian, commercial rather than exclusively national. The Anglo-German Naval Treaty of June 1935 gave a rude shock to the northern states, for it acknowledged the supremacy of the German Fleet in Baltic waters. In December 1935 the Finnish Prime Minister, Kivimäki (whose long-lived ministry—1932–36—depended on Social-Democratic votes, though he himself was a

Progressive), invited the Prime Ministers of the three Scandinavian countries to attend a conference of Social-Democratic leaders in Helsinki. The keynote of the meeting was sounded by the Swedish Premier: "Those in our northern countries," he said, "who do not regard northern co-operation as axiomatic can be soon counted. We are situated close to each other, we have a common history and a similar culture, and in the course of development towards a richer life within each of our countries the bonds which unite us have been made ever stronger. In times of anxiety and danger the feeling of solidarity has been especially apparent. The declaration of a full acceptance of the Scandinavian peace policy by the Government of Finland has been greeted with sincere pleasure in the whole of Sweden. The peace union, which is constituted by the relations of the northern countries to each other, has nothing to do with the old policy of alliance. We stand as free peoples at each others' side in the League of Nations, with the inherent obligations common to members, but our unity gives added power to our contributions, dictated both by idealism and self-interest, to the safeguarding of peace and liberty."

The *rapprochement* with Sweden reached its closest in April 1936 when a Finnish Week was celebrated at Stockholm. It was not without its critics in Finland where the fear that the Swedo-Finns might dominate the Republic was still alive. In October 1936 Herra Kallio, then Speaker of the Diet, broadcast a speech in which he insisted that alliance with the Baltic States, and especially with Estonia, was just as natural and necessary to Finland as alliance with the Scandinavian countries. The President Svinhufvud called upon Kallio to form a ministry. The friendship of Estonia, Latvia and Lithuania might be taken for granted, but that of militarist Poland would prove more difficult to secure; her position between Germany and Soviet Russia made an open declaration of policy dangerous. Herra Holsti, who had been recalled to the Foreign Office, had to content himself with the knowledge that Poland was reviving her old friendship with France and consequently with the democratic Powers of Europe.

By 1937 Finland had realized her natural orientation in foreign affairs. She was the pivot in a group of small nations which included Denmark, Norway and Sweden on one hand, Estonia, Latvia and Lithuania on the other. This understanding between seven northern states was all the more secure for not being embodied in a formal treaty of alliance. They could never hope to withstand a determined attempt on the part of Germany or of Russia to revive an ancient hegemony in the Baltic, but their *entente* could be expected to act as a deterrent to such ambitions.

Their position from the military point of view was not reassuring. The Government of Republican Finland had never let its contribution towards armed defence sink below 12 per cent of its total expenditure, and every year the amount allocated to the Ministry of Defence was increased. In June 1932 the law enjoining compulsory military service was confirmed and the armed forces reorganized. As well as a small professional army and navy, consisting of scarcely more than officers, technicians and instructors, Finland had a conscript force consisting of all the able-bodied young men in their twenty-second year, a reserve consisting of ex-conscripts between the ages of twenty-two and forty, a frontier-guard, a coast-guard, and the formidable Civic Guard with its 100,000 trained men. In May 1938 a bill providing for special expenditure of 2,710,000,000 Finnish marks (£12,000,000) during the next seven years for completing the national defences was passed by the Diet. To raise the money an increase of 20 per cent in the income and property tax was proposed. With all this Finland could not hope to withstand a month's intensive attack by a major Power, but she hoped that it would be enough to give an assailant pause and to assure potential allies that the Republic was not relying entirely on outside help for her defence.

The Oslo Powers had no alternative to rearmament. The League of Nations had proved a broken reed: it had failed in Disarmament, failed in Sanctions, failed in Non-Intervention in Spain. All Europe was rearming in face of the German menace which loomed blacker every month after the seizure of Austria in March 1938.

Meanwhile the process of economic recovery had been going steadily forward. The basis of the restored prosperity was, as we have seen, the abandoning of the gold standard and the maintenance of the Finnish mark at a fixed parity with sterling. From the middle of 1932 onwards the Finnish mark remained at the rate of 227 to the English pound. This had three most important results. The first was the expansion of export trade to Great Britain and the other nations which comprised the sterling bloc. Exports rose in value by nearly one-half and in volume by one-sixth between 1930 and 1935; by 1937 they had exceeded the previous prosperity-peak figure of 1928 in volume and in value. Secondly, Finland was enabled by what economists call her "favourable" balance of trade to pay more than half of her outstanding foreign debts. She was exporting more than she imported and the money thus left owing to her abroad went to wipe off old scores instead of being devoted to buying goods. Alone of the nations who owed money to the United States, Finland discharged her obligations punctually and in full, a fact which was not without effect on the sympathies of American citizens. Thirdly, Finland's recovery left her with money available for capital development. New industries were established and old industries remodelled, the standard of housing, central heating and electric lighting were improved, means of communication underwent a much-needed reconstruction. It is significant that Finland was now beginning to import more goods for capital purposes than for consumption.

Everything, from the building boom in England to a succession of good harvests at home, worked together to bring about a return to prosperity. Industrial production for 1936 was higher both in volume and in value than for any previous year. By 1937 Finland was enjoying an economic condition that compared favourably even with the halcyon year 1928. State finances were healthy, the budgets from 1933 to 1937 showed a consistent surplus of revenue over expenditure. There were no serious labour disputes during those years, unless we count a strike of 4,500 metal workers in April and May 1936 which resulted in an average increase in wages of 0·90 marks per hour. Unemployment in 1937 was practically non-existent.

This recovery did not merely mean a return to pre-crisis conditions; it meant a new development in Finland's economic structure. On the one hand she had come to rely more than ever on trade with one single country—Great Britain; on the other she was not relying to anything like the old extent on trade in one single commodity. Wood and wood-products still made up some 83 per cent of her total exports, but wood in its cruder forms of round and sawn timber no longer held its old predominance. Instead of raw material Finland was exporting manufactured products: pulp, cardboard and paper, sulphate- and sulphite-cellulose were being turned out in fast increasing quantities. The annual value of pulp board and paper exports in the pre-crisis years was 28 per cent of the total exports, in 1935 it was 43·5 per cent. Thus Finland's prosperity was no longer dependent on the price of one commodity in the international market. She was progressing on the way from a raw-material-producing to a manufacturing nation. The transition could not be without its dangers: the old balance between town and country would be altered, and possibly upset, by the increased number of factory workers and by the accelerated drift to the towns; the very nature of the people would be changed if the process continued. The Government, while encouraging the process of transition, was not blind to the dangers. Every care was taken to see that the development of agriculture kept pace with that of manufactures. The success of their policy of encouraging agriculture by tariffs and subsidies can be seen from the fact that, whereas in the year 1924–28 only 60 per cent of the foodstuffs consumed were produced at home, in 1934–35 the percentage of home products reached 81. There is still plenty of land suitable for cultivation and plenty of room for improvement in the yield per acre; no doubt if it suits her commercial policy Finland can make herself self-supporting in cereal, vegetable and animal foodstuffs.

One other point must be noticed in connection with the economic recovery. The benefits of debt-reduction and capital improvement were naturally felt by the rich rather than by the poor. Bankers and shareholders prospered, substantial industrial fortunes were made, especially in cellulose, but the poor did not receive a proportionate share in the national prosperity. The revival of industry brought the unemployed back to work, but not at the old rate of pay. Wages had dropped severely between 1930 and 1932 and they rose but little during the years of recovery. Prices too had fallen during the crisis, and it is arguable that for workers employed in industry the drop in the cost of living was even greater than the drop in wages.[1] But the same cannot be said for the farm workers and the men employed in felling, carting and floating timber. The real wages they received in 1935 were still well below the 1928 level. It is not without reason that the English *Midland Bank Review*, an organ not usually solicitous for the comfort of the masses, remarked in January 1937 that "debt repayment and capital improvement, it is fully recognized, have levied a cost, in the form of the retention of a general standard of living lower than might have been justified by the actual expansion of current trade. . . . At this stage, moreover, the opinion seems to be growing that some rise in the standard of living, effected by way of wage increases, can now safely be undertaken, if indeed it is not overdue."

How high this standard of living was and how it compared with the standard of other countries will be considered in the next chapter; here we are concerned merely with the nature of the recovery that took place in the years 1932–38. That recovery, being dependent on the prosperity of Finland's neighbours and on the stability of the international situation, showed a deterioration by the middle of 1938. But, as Risto Ryti wrote in the *Baltic Times* in July, "so far there have been only very few signs worth mentioning

[1] According to figures given, with many qualifications, by the *Bank of Finland Bulletin* for December 1935 the movement of *real* wages in Industry was as follows:

1928—100   1930—110   1932—102   1935—109.

of the beginning of a depression in Finland. Unemployment has not appeared yet, foreign trade has experienced a further increase, industrial output has not fallen off to any considerable extent, home trade has remained lively and the money market is easy. But the change in the cyclical tendency is approaching us from abroad and its influence is already felt distinctly by the exporting industry."

By 1938 Finland had caught up most of the ground lost during the crisis, and had solved many of the old problems that had appeared in new forms during the early days of the Republic. The land hunger had been assuaged by the measures taken under the Lex Kallio and kindred legislation. The shameful Prohibition experiment, ended by repeal in 1932, was by 1937 almost forgotten; once the Finns were allowed to consume as much alcohol as they could pay for, their thirst slackened: the amount of alcohol consumed annually after 1932 was always lower than in any Prohibition year (with the exception of that year of distress, 1931). The differences of opinion over foreign policy seemed to be reconciled by Holsti's policy of an understanding with both the Scandinavian and the Baltic States, and relations with Soviet Russia were actually more cordial in 1937 than they had ever been before, for in that year the Finnish Foreign Minister paid his first official visit to Moscow and seemed not dissatisfied with the result.

Even the eternal language controversy seemed to be losing some of its bitterness. Gradually the size of the Swedish-speaking minority was declining: in 1920 it numbered 11 per cent of the population, in 1930 only 9·8 per cent. The proportion of important posts held by the Swedo-Finns was declining rather more rapidly. In 1920, one in four of the students at Helsinki University were

Swedish-speaking, in 1930 only one in five. At the Presidential elections of February 1937 Kyösti Kallio beat the unfortunate Ståhlberg by a single vote and so Finland found herself with a President who until a few years ago was unable to speak Swedish.[1] There was no real protest. It seemed that the policy of treating a national minority with generosity was having its reward. Time was taking the sting out of the old quarrel.

The class controversy remained, as it remained in every country in the world—even, we are told, in the Soviet Union—but it was no longer acute as it had been during the war years and the years of crisis. Another slump, and it might break out again, but meanwhile there were no alarming signs of discontent. The Fascist movement which had gained such sweeping successes in 1930 had lost its sting. Lapua was still a nest of authoritarians, buzzing with yellow-faced, black-clothed Pietists. Pastor Kares, now old and ailing, still thundered from his pulpit, and Kosola's red house on the bridge over the river was still pointed out with veneration as the place where a great movement was hatched; but in Finland as a whole the Lapuans after eight years were described by every class as "fanatical"—the most damning of political epithets. The IKL drew its support from neither Capital nor Labour. It claimed that 90 per cent of the Lutheran clergy were in its favour; for the rest it relied for its votes on the class which in England would be called Retired Colonels, and on Pietists and on hystericals

[1] Svinhufvud offered himself for re-election as a non-Party candidate. He was defeated but in no sense discredited. In retirement "dear old Pekka" was still the Grand Old Man of Finland. He was in full possession of his faculties. The *Daily Telegraph* on 14 May, 1937, noted: "Acknowledged as one of Europe's expert shots, Mr. Svinhufvud, the ex-President of Finland, has just won a shooting contest with an aggregate of 601 points, his nearest rival scoring 583."

with Russophobia. At the 1936 elections the IKL retained its fourteen seats. In 1937 it had little significance except as a sort of vigilance committee for the detection of Communism. The other Fascist groups had disappeared. The Hitlerite Captain Kalsta had accepted the managership of a new State-owned hotel in the Arctic Circle and retired altogether from politics. In the Arctic Circle, too, was Kurt Wallenius, as manager of a fishing company. Visitors to Petsamo in 1937 commented on his German appearance, and on his youthfulness.

The Communists, for their part, seemed to have accepted political extinction. The more moderate had found a place in the Social Democratic party, the more extreme remained baffled by the now undeniable fact that no programme that savoured of Russia could hope for a following in any class in nationalist Finland. The Social Democrats remained the largest party in the Diet, increasing their number of seats by five at the general election of July 1936. They held five of the thirteen seats in the Coalition Cabinet of 1937 (there were five Agrarians, two Progressives and one Concentrationist). The course seemed set for a general levelling of class distinctions.

Finland during these post-crisis years has been in the fine flower of her growth. It may be, as Communists would have us believe, that this is but the forerunner of a revolutionary period; it may be that this period of expanding capitalism, this transition from a raw-material-producing to a manufacturing country will be followed by a period of sated markets, industrial strife, Fascism, war and decline. Or it may be that this is but a prelude to a period of general prosperity, peace and mature culture in Finland. The answer is in the womb of time.

CHAPTER 10

THE CONDITION OF THE PEOPLE

"Come tell me how you live," I cried,
"And what it is you do!"
LEWIS CARROLL

ECONOMIC slumps and booms make unsatisfactory reading. When all the trends have been followed, all the statistics scanned, the reader must be left in almost complete ignorance of the life of the people that they purport to describe. How do the Finnish people live? It may be well to avoid generalization for the moment and take actual examples.

In the late summer of 1937 the present writer visited three Finnish farms. Let us call them Rautala, Simola and Toivala, and hope that they are not untypical of the small, the medium-sized and the large farm respectively.

Rautala lies in a clearing in the birch woods in the hill- and lake-country of central Finland. There are nearly twenty acres of cultivated land under oats, rye, fodder crops and potatoes and four times as many of forest. The farm buildings look like a miniature village. The newest and most carefully tended is the bath-house, a trim wooden hut with paved floor and a new iron stove covered with small stones on which water is sprinkled to make steam for the bath when the stove is heated. The largest is the shippen. It too has stone floors, strewn with broken birch-bark in the cow stalls, with straw in the pigsties, with hay in the horse's box. All these, sties, stalls and stable, are in one room, as it were, separated into compartments by poles, so that in the winter the animals live together in the same Noah's Ark. At present they are out in the fields, the horse, the six cows, the two sows and the six thin sheep. The farm-house itself is a low log building, painted the conventional red and roofed with wooden tiles. Rag rugs lead through the vestibule into the living-room; it is low-raftered, vast, with a stone oven-stove covering one corner, beds in another, a trestle in the third, rough wooden utensils on the table, saws and axes hanging on the walls. That stove must be twelve feet by twelve (the bigger the stove is the longer it holds the heat and the more comfortable the house); it is the pride of the household, which consists of the master and the mistress, two serving-maids and an old labourer who sleeps on the trestle. The master of Rautala is not a farmer; he works at a munition factory twelve miles away through the forests, coming home every evening in the summer and for week-ends in the winter months. If his sons were at home he could give up his work, get rid of his servants and live on the farm, which could be made to support his family; but his sons are away in the towns, one a fully-fledged lawyer, the other still working for his teachers' examinations. They come home at Christmas and for the June holiday, and there is great feasting at Rautala.

For the rest of the year the work of the farm goes on quietly and without remission. The farm is almost self-supporting. The girls look after the animals, milk, separate and churn and do the housework. The mistress is responsible for the clothing and food; she puts the wool of their own sheep through every process from cleaning to weaving and fashioning; she cuts the flax and makes up her own linen into sheets and towels and shifts; she prepares and cooks the rare meat, digs and cuts the vegetables and bakes the bread. At Rautala they use their own flour. Behind the sauna there is an old threshing barn: planks six feet from the floor make an open platform where the new-cut oats are laid in August, and sunk below the floor is a stone fireplace with logs burning—pine and birch. It is bricked over, but a vent is left open so that the smoke comes out into the barn and hangs in a thick cloud under the platform, drying the oats thoroughly. After a few days the fire is put out and the oats taken down and threshed by hand with a wooden flail roughly hinged with a wooden peg. At present the barn is being used by a neighbouring farmer; for this he pays the master of Rautala one man's work for one day. Nothing in this method of threshing, and probably nothing in the rent, has been changed for centuries. The master of Rautala remembers grinding his own grain (there are a pair of grindstones in the yard bearing the date 1720) but to-day he sends it away to the co-operative mill in the centre of the parish.

For meals family and servants alike sit round the heavy table in the living-room. There are usually potatoes boiled in their jackets, followed by messes of junket and curdled milk. The old labourer eats noisily, using no implement but his clasp knife and belching his appreciation. The girls manipulate forks after the manner of the mistress. There is little talking, the meals being taken almost in silence, sacramentally. The only luxury—beyond butter and fruit in season, which are hardly luxuries since they come from the farm—is coffee, which is drunk three or four times a day; if the conversation ever wanders beyond local affairs it is by way of speculation on the cause of the fluctuations of the price of coffee. Sugar, books and tobacco are almost the only necessities that Rautala does not produce for itself.

The work of the farm goes on with its own endless rhythm. Of leisure as such there is hardly any conception; it is a ritual in the same way as labour. On Saturday afternoon the *sauna* is heated, and water brought from the well. (The well is deep but has no winding gear. A twelve-foot upright pole holds a thinner twenty-foot pole in its fork. The cross-pole has a bucket hanging from one end, the other is weighted down with a stone. To get water, swing the stone-end up till the bucket dips in the well, then swing back. It is a child's work.) Nobody ever misses his bath. First the men shut themselves in the *sauna* and emerge pink as lobsters to splash their bodies with cold water and dry themselves, if it is summer, in the sun. Then it is the women's turn, mistress and girls together. On Sunday mornings the necessary farm-work is done more slowly, after which men and women dress in their best and take a stroll, or perhaps once a month make the long journey to the parish church. In the summer, with all the work of the fields to be crowded into three months, there is rarely time for church, but in winter it is easier. Darkness forcibly cuts down the working hours and there is less to be done. The old labourer has his work cut out felling the birch-wood at the bottom of the rye field; he succeeds in bringing a few more yards under cultivation every year. In the evenings he is busy with the manifold crafts of harness and sledge making. The women have more time on their hands; even when the routine has been got through and the clothes made for the next year, there is time to spare. It is fortunate when country women in Finland can arrange to bear their children during the winter months.

It would be easy to sentimentalize Rautala—the still pine-scented morning with the cow's bell sounding like the noise of some far-distant smithy, some forest Ilmarinen's hammer on the anvil, and the girl's yodelling cry as she goes out barefoot and bucket in hand after the straying cattle. The summer of 1937 was good. If it had been wet and cold and the crops bad the girl would have been away to Jyväskylä, thirty miles to the south, in search of a servant's job in a flat in the town.

Rautala must be an almost typical small farm. It is not unusual for a smallholder to be a factory worker for a few months in the year; or, to put it another way, it is not unusual for a factory worker to buy a small farm on borrowed money. For the master of Rautala to have one son in the legal and one in the teaching profession is nothing out of the way: where else are lawyers and schoolmasters to be recruited from?

There is a very different air about Simola. It lies a score of miles inland from Turku, in the oldest inhabited part of Finland, and includes about a hundred acres of ploughland and pasture and another hundred of forest. The master of Simola is a stocky bright-eyed man in the middle thirties, with the bridgeless nose and wide mouth that are so common in Finland. Simola has been owned by his family for only a hundred years, but it has been built up from nothing and he hopes to leave his sons a really prosperous estate. He is immensely proud of his achievements. The farm buildings are shabby, the gates falling to pieces, he has installed neither telephone nor electric light, though both are cheap, but he is unconcerned about these deficiencies, being the kind of man who grudges any capital expenditure. He has not realized that borrowing for productive purposes is a very different thing from borrowing for consumption: borrowing, in his eyes, is shameful as well as dangerous; he regards his bank as a safe-deposit, not as a moneylender. Yet his herd of cows—a cross between Ayrshires and the small Finnish breed—without being prizewinners have an exceptionally good milk yield. He seems to be able to get a better crop of sugar beet (for which there is a Government subsidy) out of his acres than any other farmer in the neighbourhood.

The master of Simola is a progressive farmer. He keeps books that would be a credit to a professional accountant. And he is particularly interested in the new A.I.V. method of preserving fodder. For this purpose he has built a circular bin some twelve feet deep and eight in diameter, very beautifully made with narrow planks, freshly tarred. The bin is only just completed. Next month he will pile in the fodder—clover, beet-tops and the like—and soak it with the A.I.V. chemical liquid which preserves food value. For a medium-sized farm this A.I.V. plant is a remarkable achievement. Apart from this, his reputation rests solely on his skill and industry. He is a hard taskmaster. The three labourers are kept well at work to earn their thirty marks a day, but it must be a satisfaction to them to know that the master works harder and for longer hours.

The Simola farm-house is small, neat and overcrowded. A tiny bedroom, a small iron-stoved kitchen and a sitting-room that is not much bigger, is all the accommodation for master, mistress and four children. The sitting-room is crowded with dresser, table and chairs of painted wood; the embroidered covers and loosely woven curtains, the cactus plants and fly-papers give a sense of stuffiness which is not relieved by the windows, whose edges are still sealed with paper pasted on for the previous winter. Here the master of Simola entertains his guests to morning coffee. There are five kinds of biscuits and cakes made by his wife of flour, sugar, eggs, butter and milk in varying proportions. There are no currants or sultanas in them, no candied peel or icing, but they are an obvious luxury, for the children fidget in the background hardly able to wait until the guests have gone. The mistress herself waits, standing behind the master and never taking her seat at the table. The master discusses her openly with the guests; she will not have another child, he thinks, yet Finland needs children; why, he cannot get an extra hand to help with the harvest. Looking at the master of Simola one realizes why Communism has met such stubborn resistance in Finland.

It is not far from Simola to Toivala. The road runs for a mile through the cornfields, twists through a village with red painted houses, white school and an assortment of co-operative shops, runs on over the crest of a low hill and forks into an avenue of birch trees. At the end of the avenue is the Toivala house, a pretentious wooden building, gabled and terraced and painted a light grey. Within there is a huge vestibule cloakroom, a study full of maps, desks, files and telephones, and a suite of guest-rooms. The family quarters are apart from the rest, for this is a big farm. The main guest-room is like a stage-set. White painted chairs in a sort of peasant-baroque are set stiffly round a polished table; there is china behind glass, two grandfather clocks (neither in working order) and rugs hanging on the walls. There are also some regrettable landscapes in oils. After this it is a surprise to meet the master of Toivala—an old badger of a man, with pointed nose, shrewd little eyes and close grey hair *en brosse*. He is rich and successful and owns

192

400 acres of ploughland and 10 of orchard and kitchen
garden, but he employs no bailiff or manager or book-
keeper, though he is past middle age; he runs the farm himself and will continue to do so until he breaks down or dies.

The Toivala fields lie on a gentle slope facing south over
the broad plain towards Turku. They are not cut into ten-
metre strips by the open ditches that one sees almost everywhere in Finland; the drains are underground and the fields
stretch smooth and unbroken as in Wiltshire. Now, in mid-
August, most of the harvest is in, though a motor-tractor is
still at work cutting the last corner. The tractor is driven
by the master's son and heir; in a year or two he will go
away to an agricultural college, but he must get his experi-
ence of farmwork first (shades of Wye, where there is
hardly a student who has known a year's practical work!).
He is careful with the tractor; a machine like that should last
ten years, otherwise in a country where labour is so cheap
it is not worth its purchase.

Over in the big barn they are threshing with a new Siva
machine. This costs next to nothing to work, though the
electric power is brought from Imatra, hundreds of miles
away. Horses stand quietly in the din beside their laden
carts while men load the wheat into the maw of the machine.
The master of Toivala watches the grain pouring out into
sacks, the straw being elevated up into stacks, the chaff
being blown out of a side vent. He smiles; it is a good crop.

Over in the cowshed the girls are busy milking. The
Toivala herd are Ayrshires, which give a bigger yield but
consume more food than the Finnish breed. The cowshed
is dark—they whitewash it only once a year, in the autumn
—and the girls work bare-footed in the muck. There is little
fuss about cleanliness in Finland, where there has rarely

been a case of bovine tuberculosis. In spite of its big herd, Toivala neither separates nor churns: the milk is taken direct by lorry to the co-operative creamery. Toivala's whole economy depends on co-operation; the master has hardly any dealings with private firms.

Like the master of Simola, and in spite of the wide differences in their financial positions, he is a member of the Agrarian Party. The small farmer and the big have common interests and there is no political and hardly any social barrier between them. Gentlemen farmers who work their land for a hobby and landlords who have agents to administer their estates would no doubt be Concentrationists, but they are exceptional even in the Turku district. In the neighbouring district of Vaasa there are not a dozen of them in all. The master of Toivala is a typical rich landowner. He has been in the fields since seven o'clock. Now it is eleven-thirty—the men's dinner-hour. He adjusts the controls of the Siva machine, ties up a sack of grain, calls to his son on the tractor and trudges in through the gate in the high yew hedge of his private garden to lunch.

The Toivala labourers get 30 marks a day, the same as the men at Simola. Two-and-eight a day and nothing found—it is not much. But they live in cottages that they have built themselves, they have a vegetable plot and perhaps a cow, and with food prices so low (herrings in brine cost 8 marks a kilogram—about 4d. a pound—and calves' liver 12 marks a kilogram—about 6d. a pound) they are not badly off. Those of the labourers who live-in get 350 marks a month and all found. The master of Toivala admits that this is too little; he has promised to raise their wages by 100 marks this winter. Evidently he has difficulty in keeping his men. The unmarried workman is a rolling stone. He works on the

POPULATION

Compiled from official statistics of births, deaths, etc., as quoted in the Bank of Finland Monthly Bulletin of September 1929 & August 1932.

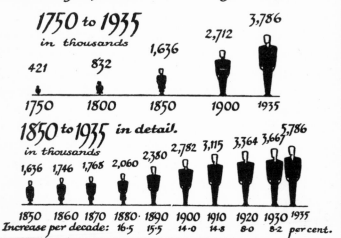

1750 to 1935

in thousands

421	832	1,636	2,712	3,786
1750	1800	1850	1900	1935

1850 to 1935 in detail.

in thousands

1,636	1,746	1,768	2,060	2,380	2,782	3,115	3,364	3,667	3,786
1850	1860	1870	1880	1890	1900	1910	1920	1930	1935

Increase per decade: 16·5 15·5 14·0 14·8 8·0 8·2 per cent.

OCCUPATIONS

Number engaged in Agriculture estimated to be 2 millions.

IN 1934

Numbers engaged in Industry 162,000.

Timber, Paper, Pulp, etc.

Textiles & Clothing.
MachineryShops.
Foodstuffs.
Stone, Clay, Glass, etc.

Percentages 55 18 14 7 6 of Industry.

land in the summer and in the forests in the winter, going from farm to farm and from lumber-camp to camp until he finds a master and conditions that suit him. Then he will marry perhaps and settle down, finding a farmer who will provide a cottage-plot and take him on as a day-labourer, or following the timber rafts to a factory and taking employment as an industrial worker there. In either case he will be saving up, no doubt to buy a small farm like Rautala.

Supposing that he takes the road to a factory, how does he live? As like as not it will be one of the factories of the Enso-Gutzeit-Tornator concern which, with its 25,000 employees, is one of the biggest in Finland. We may imagine that he goes to the headquarters factory at Enso. It is in the pine-forests in South-East Finland, thirty miles north of Viipuri. The Saimaa water-system taps the richest forest areas of Finland, floating the logs down to Enso and floating them on again to the ports; the hydro-electric stations on the adjacent rapids provide the power for the sulphite mill, the sulphate mill, the bleaching plant, the pulp mill and the paper mill, the chlorine laboratory and the water-glass factory, that have sprung up amid the pine forests at Enso. It is a surprising colony. The office block looks like the town hall of a progressive county borough, but there is no sign of a town. The houses are hidden in the trees, here a block of flats, here a string of two-storey houses, there a group of cabins. All the people employed at Enso live within three miles of their work. One in four of the homes are owned by the Enso company; they used to build blocks of flats but found them unsuitable to rural conditions, and are concentrating now on two-storey houses in which each storey is a self-containing flat with a large living-room, a bedroom and a kitchen. For these the company charges less than an economic rent, but even so the rent averages a quarter of the tenant's wage.

The man who is taken on as an unskilled labourer at Enso gets 3 marks an hour and works his way up, as his skill increases, to a rate of 10 or 11 marks an hour. The working-week is of 48 hours: thus the wage-rates—144 to 528 marks a week—compare favourably with the farm-labourer's 180. But in reality no comparison is possible because Enso is a society in itself. The nearest English equivalent is the Bourneville works, though Enso pride themselves on doing more for their workers than Messrs. Cadbury. They provide hospitals and maternity homes, district nurses and children's welfare centres, athletic grounds, swimming-baths and playgrounds; they run dramatic societies, libraries and lecture-courses; they maintain a free boarding school with a one-year course for boys in their sixteenth year who have left the elementary school and are too young for employment. They pay the full premiums of sickness, old age and disablement insurance and two-thirds of the premiums on optional insurance policies for workers' families. The whole organization has a patriarchal feeling about it in spite of its immensity and its modernity.[1] Families live their whole lives, work-time and leisure, under the Enso company. Whether the advantages of this outweigh the disadvantages is open to argument. Among the former is the feeling of security and community, the knowledge that the company will not let a servant's family go to the wall and will give its members preference over outsiders when taking on new

[1] The company began as the Gutzeit saw-mill in Kotka in 1872. In 1911 it absorbed the Enso concern and in 1919 the controlling interest in the combine was acquired by the Finnish State which now owns 87 per cent of the share capital. The share of the combine in Finland's total export trade is about 10 per cent.

hands; among the latter is a certain loss of liberty which is involved in all these welfare organizations. Enso employs no trade unionists. The man who likes to feel that he has no connection with his employer outside his working hours, and the man who looks for solidarity with the working-class as a whole rather than with the employees and employers in his immediate concern, should avoid Enso and go to one of the towns.

The town worker still comprises only a small proportion of the Finnish working-class. The percentage of the population living in towns in 1800 was only 5, in 1900 it was 12, in 1935 nearly 20. From many points of view the town worker is a privileged being. In England we are apt to think of him as dragging out his existence amid dirt and din in a slum, and not seeing open country more than two or three times in the year. In Finland there are no slums, very little coal-dirt and hardly any din except that made by wooden wheels rattling over cobbled streets.[1] The reason is not far to seek. There is no dirt or din because the motive power of industry is electricity, which makes neither. There are no slums because there are no old towns in Finland. Turku and Viipuri are ancient foundations, but they were almost entirely rebuilt after fires in the eighteenth century. To-day Turku is a pleasant little provincial town with an academic air about it. The buildings are almost all of wood and the streets are laid out on a rectangular plan; the river that runs through the city provides free bathing and almost free boating, and in the summer evenings the proletariat takes its leisure listening to the bands in the parks by the river-side or lounging on one of the islands in the archipelago.

[1] One prime source of urban din, the motor-horn, was forbidden by law in 1934, with the result that road accidents immediately fell by half.

Viipuri has a less orderly air. It has been rebuilt in stone and resembles a German city more than a Scandinavian, but the new quarters have been carefully and spaciously planned. Neither Turku nor Viipuri has a population exceeding 70,000. From the centre of either, open country or water can be reached by a penny bus-ride in almost any direction.

The only large town in Finland is Helsinki with its 270,000 inhabitants. There if anywhere one would expect to find bad living conditions. Yet there are no slums because the town is scarcely more than a century old and was intended from the beginning as an administrative and industrial capital. Town-planning was undertaken from the first, the big companies building flats for their workers at the same time as they built their factories, the town council scheduling definite areas for development and financing schemes to help town workers to build summer cabins within easy cycling distance of their jobs. The council even bought islands in the bay to be set aside as bathing resorts, whither people could be transported from the centre of the town at a charge of a penny or twopence. Yet Helsinki has not altogether succeeded in avoiding overcrowding. The average number of inhabitants per room was 1·7 in 1920 and 1·5 in 1930. This is far too high, though it compares well with Glasgow, for example, or with several English cities. Rents are far too high. A worker's modern one-room flat can hardly be found for less than 150 marks a week (which includes heat, light, water and rates). This will run away with nearly a third of the unskilled worker's income, but for the rest living is not expensive in the towns. Recreation, at least in its outdoor forms, costs very little, and food is cheap. A good meal of milk, meat and vegetables and a sweet can be obtained in a clean and comfortable restaurant for the equivalent of about fivepence. In many cases the worker is attracted to the towns by the possibility of obtaining better food. Paradoxically enough, the problems of feeding and housing are more acute in the country districts than in the towns. So is the problem of over-work. The bakers, still a sweated industry in most countries, are protected by a law passed as early as 1908 fixing a maximum working week of forty-eight hours, and forbidding night work; and the eight-hour day law, passed in 1917, applies to all industries with the exception of agriculture.

After all this, what level does the general standard of living in Finland reach? The impression of the traveller who makes a casual tour of the northern countries will no doubt be that it is rather below the standard of Denmark and Sweden, and distinctly above that of the Baltic States and the Soviet Union. Casual impressions are often right, but they convince nobody; we must attempt a more exact estimate.

The average wage of factory workers during 1936 was 7·45 marks per hour, that of workers in the saw mills and lumber camps 6·03 marks and that of workers in the foundries 5·81 marks per hour. The average weekly wage of an industrial labourer can be taken as 270 marks (about 24s.).

Wages, then, are low in Finland. On the other hand prices are low—lower for essential commodities than in any other European country except Estonia, and it is no use knowing what wages the average Finn is paid unless we know what he can buy with them. He can evidently buy sugar and coffee in comparatively large quantities, for the average consumption of those luxuries *per capita* is larger than in Germany, France and Italy, though not so large as in England and the Scandinavian countries. But how much better off is the Finn than the average German, for instance? How much worse off than the average Englishman?

The difficulty is to find a standard of comparison. The British working man can afford little fresh milk or butter, yet has enough money for cigarettes and the cinema. The Finn lives on milk and butter, yet has less to spend on cinema and tobacco. How can the two be compared?

The best basis for comparison is that of the economist Engels, who discovered that rich and poor devote approximately the same proportion of their incomes to rent, heating and lighting, but that the poor devote a higher proportion to food and a lower proportion to "sundries." The standard of living is therefore highest in those countries in which the ratio of expenditure on food is least and the ratio of sundry expenditure highest. (It is a mad world in which the man who spends proportionately least on necessities is called "well off," but it is the economists' world and we must put up with it.) A calculation of working-class expenditure on this basis was published by the International Labour Office in November 1933 and August 1934; it shows that the Finns' standard of living was higher than that of the Germans, for instance, or of the Poles, Czechs, Swedes or Irish.[1]

[1] Unfortunately the I.L.O. figures do not all relate to the same year.

| | | | | Per cent of wages spent on: | |
Country			Year	Food	Sundries
Finland ..	..	..	1928	43·4	26·8
Germany	..	..	1927–28	46·3	22·8
Holland ..	..	..	1923	43·4	23·5
Norway ..	..	..	1927–28	44·3	22·9
Sweden ..	..	..	1923	45·3	23·1

Continued at foot of page 202

In comparing living conditions in Finland with conditions in neighbouring countries we are handicapped by lack of figures for Russia. Obviously it would be pointless to measure Finns against the citizens of the U.S.S.R. as a whole; only Russians of the north-western districts are in any way comparable, and here statistics of wages, expenditure and health are not to be procured. We must rely on the general impressions of observers. Not one of these has ever doubted that the working-classes are materially much better off in Finland than in Russia. They are to-day, as they have been for centuries, better fed, better clad, better housed, better equipped and better educated. Yet it may still, of course, be true that, as Marxists would have us believe, they are an exploited proletariat, deprived by the capitalists of their rightful share of the national wealth and cut off by their rulers from the classless religion in whose service alone is perfect freedom.

The gap between rich and poor in Finland is vastly wider than in the Soviet Union. There are still 827 estates of 250 acres and more of ploughland; in other words one-thousandth of the population holds one-fifteenth of the arable land.

Yet this gap between rich and poor is not so wide as in

Country			Year	Per cent of wages spent on: Food	Sundries
Denmark	..	..	1922	40·5	25·0
China	..	..	1926–27	72·2	1·7
Japan	..	..	1926–27	39·8	26·1
India	..	..	1926	57·9	12·7
Ireland	..	..	1922	57·1	13·0
U.S.A.	..	..	1929	33·4	20·3
Poland	..	..	1927–29	63·2	12·7
Switzerland	..	..	1922	49·5	16·5
Czechoslovakia		..	1927–29	55·6	19·5
Estonia	..	..	1925	57·9	9·6

West European countries. There is equality of opportunity in Finland in so far that secondary and university education is free and admission open to talent. If the standard of living of the workers is by international comparison high, that of the rich is low. The clerical and professional classes are comfortably situated but by no means wealthy. The salary of the higher civil servant, measured in money, is less than a fifth of that of his opposite number in the United Kingdom. As a writer in the *Finland Year Book* of 1935 says: "A skilled workman, a business employee with a secondary-school education and a civil servant of the lower ranks live in outwardly fairly similar circumstances, and the standard of living of even the highest ranked Government officials differs from that of the persons mentioned chiefly in the respect that they can afford roomier living quarters and spend rather more money on interests of an artistic or other cultural nature." The industrial and commercial classes, on the other hand, have a few very wealthy men at the top. Six persons in Finland own property worth more than 30,000,000 marks (£140,000). But only six. The members of the Stockholm Chamber of Commerce could buy up the Helsinki magnates many times over; there has been no Kreuger in Finnish history.

Living conditions, however good, are not satisfactory without security, and in this respect Finland lags behind the nations of Western Europe. There is no insurance against unemployment. It is true that to-day, in 1938, there is no considerable unemployment, but the present boom can not be expected to last for ever. What is more, there is no really powerful trade union organization to look after the interests of the workers. Twice a great trade union movement has been launched, only to founder on each occasion on political rocks. In 1918, when the movement had 160,000 members, it lent its support to direct political action and was dissolved by the White Government after the civil war; in 1930 when a new organization had been built up with a membership of nearly 100,000, it was dissolved in the Lapua panic. After the slump the movement had to start again from the beginning. Three new bodies were founded, the Central Federation, the Independent Labour League, and the National Trade Union Organization, but their combined membership in 1934 was under 90,000 and they were incapacitated by political cleavages from combined action. To-day the printing and some smaller trades have collective agreements with their workers but the timber and other big industries have none. Whether collective agreements will become general in the future will depend on the power of the Social Democratic leaders to control the unions until they win more general support.

Other forms of insurance for workers' security have also been a long time coming. Not until May 1937 did the President sanction a law providing old age and disablement pensions, to come into operation at the beginning of 1940. Premiums are to be paid into the insurance fund by the State, the local authorities and the employers. The employers are entitled to deduct for this purpose 1 per cent of every employee's wage for the first five years and 2 per cent in subsequent years; his own contribution must amount to at least half of these deductions. Out of the fund the State is to pay to persons who are disabled or over sixty-five years of age pensions varying according to the strength of the fund and the amount paid in premiums by the pensioner. How this law will work out in practice remains to be seen. Meanwhile the indigent are dependent upon private charity and the attentions of the Poor Law authorities in parishes and boroughs. The treatment meted out by these latter varies immensely. At the worst it is not too bad. We may take for example the relief work done in the town of Turku which, as an old and declining city and a centre of conservatism, can hardly be supposed to be above the average.

Of the 70,000 people of Turku 2,268 received some sort of outdoor relief every month during 1936. In most cases the relief took the form of food-tickets which gave the recipients the right to buy foodstuffs up to a certain value from a list of specified commodities. The tickets were presentable only at the Council shop where the goods, besides being of guaranteed quality, were sold at prices slightly below those prevailing in the open shops. Besides this outdoor relief some 650 old people found accommodation in the workhouse. This ungainly structure was put up in the 1880's but has been modernized with considerable ingenuity. Most of the inmates lived in wards containing four beds, but there were a few "family flats" inhabited by man and wife. Neither the buyers in the shop nor the inmates of the workhouse seemed galled by, much less ashamed of, their dependence. A comfortable garrulity pervaded both institutions, the housewives chattering with the shop-girls and the old people in the workhouse grumbling amiably to their attendants. The Finns have known too much poverty in the past to resent public "charity" at this stage.

Neither housing nor poverty is the most serious social problem that Finland has to solve; the most serious problem concerns public health. The general standard of health is not by any means bad: of the young men who came under the Conscription Law in 1927 over 64 per cent were passed as physically fit for active service. This is a high figure and it has increased fairly steadily: in 1936, 78 per cent were passed. But there is one alarming item on the list of diseases causing exemption: of every 100 men inspected nine were suffering from tuberculosis in 1927, seven in 1936. The most important task that lies before Finland in the future is to reduce the ravages of this disease.

To the question "Why is there so much tuberculosis in Finland?" there is no really satisfactory answer. People who happen to dislike the Finns say that it is because they are a "bad stock." Social reformers (in other countries) say that it is the result of overcrowding. The men whose business is to lead the crusade against the disease in Finland say that the tubercle, like other germs, comes in waves and that at present that particular wave covers eastern Europe. The map of Europe, with each country shaded according to the incidence of the disease, shows light in the west, rather darker in the centre and black in the east. For example, in 1935 there were 7·4 cases of tuberculosis in the United Kingdom per 10,000 of the population, 8·5 in Sweden, but 18·5 in Finland, 18·0 in Poland and 18·2 in Roumania. Between these three eastern nations there is nothing in common, neither race, climate nor living conditions; between Sweden and Finland there is a great deal in common: how, then, explain the incidence of the disease except by the wave theory? A map of the incidence in the various parishes of Finland itself seems to confirm this theory. Ten years ago the blackest areas were along the west coast, to-day they are in central Finland. This, then, would seem to be the only explanation of the plague with which the nation is cursed, this and the fact that between 1809 and 1917 Russia allowed them no money to combat the disease and that in the first ten years of independence the Government had no resources to spare for it.

To-day the campaign against tuberculosis is well under way. In half the parishes of Finland there is a State-supported service of free tests by whole-time travelling doctors. In 1936 they tested 133,000 people for tuberculosis, sending those who showed positive reactions on to the hospitals for X-ray examination. Cows were also tested; when the animals reacted positively it meant that there was infection among the farm-hands, for bovine tuberculosis is almost non-existent in Finland. By these methods it is hoped to check the disease in its early stages; within the next twenty years the free-test service will be extended to every parish in the country.

At the same time a great deal of money and energy is being devoted to the treatment of the disease. The initiative is left to private societies, which can get from the State three-quarters of the cost of the building and equipment of hospitals and 14 marks per patient per day, on condition that they take 50 per cent of their patients without charge. Some of the finest of the new buildings in Finland are hospitals set up under this system for the treatment of tuberculosis. Of these Paimion Parantola is a good example. It is a vast eight-storey building designed by Alvar Aalto in the functionalist style. Long balconies run the length of the south fronts, and behind them the wards, mostly of two beds each, lie open to the sun. It must be a strange place for farm-hands from Rautala to find themselves in, among the steel bedtables, the semi-circular wardrobes, the pastel-shades of the long corridors and all the quiet impersonal efficiency. The average stay of a patient in Paimion Parantola lasts only six months. They go back to their wooden cabins and to their work in the cow-shed or the forest, and return, all too often, to the hospital if the disease renews its attack, for there is as yet little provision for after-care. There is a limit to what human ingenuity can do against tuberculosis, and a more obvious limit to the resources that can be devoted to its prevention and cure by a small and new nation.

CHAPTER 11

CIVILIZATION AND CULTURE TO-DAY

"L'arbre finlandais pousse des racines jusque dans le désert
glacé, mais, aux pointes de sa ramure, s'épanouissent les
fleurs les plus délicates de notre civilisation."

GEORGES DUHAMEL

AFTER nine hundred years of subjection and twenty years
of independence, what manner of civilization have the
people of Finland forged for themselves?

The answer must depend, of course, on definitions. To
nine Englishmen out of ten civilization connotes three
qualities: cleanliness, honesty and kindness. The Turks are
neither clean, honest nor kind, therefore they are uncivi-
lized; the English are all three, therefore they are civilized.
What, then, of the Finns? No traveller returns from Finland
without a tale of the striking cleanliness of the Finland Line
steamers, of the quays, the streets, the hotels and, above all,
of the people—the people whose oldest national institution
is the steam bath. No traveller but is struck by their honesty
and kindness; one wearies of the anecdotes about the
waitress who returned a tip of 10 marks (a shilling) on the
ground that the gentleman must have mistaken the coin for
1 mark (a penny), and about the peasant family who gave
a night's hospitality to a stranger speaking not one word
of their language, and refused to hear of payment.[1] By this

---

[1] One example of these anecdotes, if only because it dates from 1789.
Joseph Acerbi wrote: "Having crossed the river at this place our guides
informed us that we had no further occasion for them, and that we might

definition the Finns must be among the most highly civilized people in the world. It may be presumed, therefore, that the definition is inadequate.

It has often been said that the civilization of a country may be judged by the status of its womenfolk. In 1906 when Finland gave women equal political rights with men, foreigners of every hue looked on the experiment with ill-disguised amusement. It was generally thought to be certain to fail. All manner of difficulties were predicted: the women would not trouble to use their votes; those who did would vote exclusively for female candidates; they would all vote for one of the old parties, or else for a new feminist party. The 1907 elections gave the lie to all these forecasts. The proportion of female electors to use their votes was only slightly lower than that of male—60 per cent as compared with 70 per cent. The women did not vote exclusively for female candidates, as is shown by the fact that only fourteen women were elected to the new Diet. (Incidentally the number of women members has never exceeded twenty. To-day it is seventeen.) They did not form a separate party and their support was divided among the existing parties in rough proportion to those parties' general popularity. What is more, the conduct of the women members in the Diet was exemplary. Mechelin himself said: "Many of the questions brought up by them had not received proper attention from the men. Among the questions of reform which have been taken up by the Diet on the initiative of women members, the following may be mentioned: the property rights of women, the raising of

pursue our journey without the smallest apprehension. They instantly left us, without waiting for any sort of recompense for their services; and when we called them back and offered them money, they seemed astonished that we should think of rewarding them."

the marriage age for women from fifteen to seventeen, the improvement of the legal position of illegitimate children, the establishment of maternity insurance for very poor women, the appointment of women sanitary inspectors, the setting aside of funds for the promotion of public morality, the extension of the right of women to hold public offices. The above examples show that our women representatives have especially concerned themselves with those spheres in which women usually have a closer insight into existing evils than men. This is not feminism, for the measures proposed are all of a universally important nature." When British statesmen were obstinately warding off the umbrellas and hat-pins of suffragettes it was the Finns' turn to be amused.

A more familiar charge against the influence of Finnish women in politics is that their votes prevented the repeal of the unenforcible Prohibition law. It was argued that no party dared remove the Prohibition plank from its platform for fear of losing the female vote. If this is true it shows a bad miscalculation on the part of the political leaders, who were mostly men. For at the plebiscite of 1931 nearly twice as many women voted for the abolition of Prohibition as voted for retaining it. The number of women who voted against Prohibition was larger than the total number of men and women who voted for it.[1]

The economic equality of the sexes has also gone farther in Finland than elsewhere. Equal pay for equal work has not been accepted in principle—nor is it likely to be so long as

	Men	Women	Total
[1] For retaining Prohibition	101,502	115,667	217,169
For removing wine and beer restrictions only	6,033	4,914	10,947
For abolishing Prohibition	319,465	226,838	546,303

it is the man who is responsible for the upkeep of the family
—but in practice the disparity of wages as between men
and women is not striking. Every career except the armed
services and the priesthood is open to women, and there is
no discrimination against married women as such. Twenty
per cent of the industrial workers are women. It may be
doubted whether this proportion will be kept up. At present
Finland is in a comparatively early stage of her industrial
revolution; so far, except during short-lived crises, there
has been a shortage of labour. Employers have been eager
for labourers of either sex, and men workers have not
been jealous of women for there has been no question of
their being displaced by cheap female labour. When Finland
reaches a more advanced stage of her capitalist development
a movement may come to withdraw women from the
labour market. But at present there are no signs of it. Streets
are swept and buses conducted by women; teeth are tended
and chins shaved by women dentists and women barbers.
Women carrying hods may still be seen on the new buildings
of Helsinki, and one of the most familiar sights is the old
woman in the lace cap placidly knitting as she waits to turn
the points for the tram cars in the middle of the city.

How far it is a mark of civilization for women to carry
hods or turn tram-points is a matter of opinion. Access to
unskilled and semi-skilled industrial employment is a
doubtful advantage, but there can be no doubt of the
benefits derived by women from access to professional
work. In highly industrialized communities like Great
Britain, where so many of the housewives' tasks have been
taken out of the home, the women of the middle classes
have suddenly found themselves with time on their hands.
Where neither the baking of bread nor the making or

washing of clothes is done in the home, where the cleaning is done by electric appliances and much of the preparation of food by shops and canning factories, where the children are looked after by nursery schools and no animals are kept except as pets, there is comparatively little work left for the woman of the house to perform. What is she to do with her new-found leisure? In England the women of the bourgeoisie, after they have married and borne perhaps a couple of children, find themselves with no tradition to guide them in the use of their leisure. Most careers are closed to them, even if they happen to have the training and the taste for a career, and their education has in few cases fitted them for serious intellectual or aesthetic pursuits. They kill time with golf, tennis and bridge, with gossip, cinema-going and the cultivation of a fashionable appearance. In Finland it is the rule rather than the exception for girls of well-to-do families to study at a specialized school or at the university, where half of the undergraduates are women; after marriage and child-bearing they have no difficulty in going back to their jobs—there is no ban, for example, on married school-mistresses; and in many cases they are equipped to lead a life of cultured leisure.

These educational and occupational privileges involve certain duties. Women in Finland are responsible for their own debts. Rich women whom the divorce courts find to be guilty parties are bound to pay alimony. A number of women's voluntary organizations have been formed to undertake duties in the sphere of social services. The Martha League for instruction in the manifold crafts of house-keeping has 43,000 members among the Finnish-speaking population alone (it may be compared with the Women's Institute movement in England). There is also an organization (called after Runeberg's heroine, Lotta Svärd) affiliated to the Civic Guard, its object being "to awaken and strengthen the idea of the Civic Guard and assist the Civic Guard to defend the faith, the home and the country." In practice this means that the 72,000 Lotta Svärd women train as military clerks, nurses, cooks, laundry workers and seamstresses or work at collecting funds and distributing propaganda for the Civic Guard. They have made themselves indispensable by undertaking the catering on all occasions when big crowds are collected—sports meetings, exhibitions and song festivals. In short, the economic equality of the sexes may be said to be justified as far as the richer women are concerned. In the case of the poorer there is room for doubt.

One of the more serious problems with which Finland is faced is not unconnected with the status of women. The birth-rate is falling. During the eighteenth century the average number of births every year was 40 for every thousand of the population. Throughout the nineteenth century the figure remained in the neighbourhood of 35. But in the twentieth century it has been falling rapidly; in 1935 there were only about 20 births for every thousand people. The effects of this on the population figures are not as serious as might appear, for the death-rate has been falling almost parallel with the birth-rate. But although the population is still rising, it is rising at a decreasing pace, and before long it must begin to fall. One of the causes of the falling birth-rate is undoubtedly the employment of women in industry. It is not possible to prove this, but a comparison of the birth-rates for rural and urban areas is significant: in 1927 births in the country districts numbered 22·6 per thousand, those in the towns only 14·4. Even allowing for the larger proportion of un-married women in the towns, this difference is striking. Unless more encouragement, in the form of leisure, can be offered to urban working-class women to rear families, the population of Finland must fall rapidly before very long.

A falling birth-rate is not in itself a sign of lack of civiliza-tion; on the contrary, it is a phenomenon found in all Western nations which are commonly counted as most highly civilized. If this is a sign of civilization, Finland ranks high in this respect as well.

Let us take yet another definition. To the pedant civiliza-tion means "adept at living in a city." No one can doubt the success of the Finns in this; their solution of the prob-lems of town-planning and housing, of heating, lighting and hygiene, of sweated labour and leisure, is the envy even of the great nations of the West. Even the problem of transport and communication between town and town and town and country, which provides peculiar difficulties in Finland, has been tackled in a manner which can bear comparison with England. Helsinki is connected by daily air services with Turku, Vaasa, Tampere and Viipuri, and with Stockholm and Tallinn. Railway travel is cheap, clean and efficient. A commercial traveller can make the round of the chief towns spending successive days in each and his nights on trains where the sleeping-cars are comfortable and almost ridiculously inexpensive. A new network of Diesel-engined bus-services has linked together the larger villages, breaking down the old barriers of isolation and parochialism which have characterized Finland throughout her history.

But when all is said and done civilization is but the means of nurturing and developing the culture of a people. In China one of the finest cultures the world has known is perishing from lack of the material support of civilization, from want of the rule of law, of machinery to give effect to the will of the people, from failure to control flood and famine and the depredations of foreign capitalists. In the United Kingdom and the United States it would seem that the opposite process is at work: they enjoy "all the blessings of civilization" but those material gifts have choked their culture, so that the poets are turning to propaganda and the metaphysicians to politics in an attempt to divert the march of civilization from stamping out the ancient culture of the West.

How does the balance between culture and civilization stand in Finland? Civilization, we have suggested, is highly developed: what of Finnish culture? Has it been smothered or nurtured by progress?

To nine Englishmen out of ten culture is synonymous with education and education with book-learning. The Eskimo has a low culture because he cannot read, the Scots crofter is highly civilized because he has been, maybe, to a university. What of the Finns by this criterion? The people of Finland, including the 3,000 Lapps of the farthest north, can read and write almost without exception: less than one per cent of the people over fifteen years of age is illiterate. More books in proportion to the population are published every year in Finland than in any other country, and the largest bookshop in Europe is the Akateminen Kirjakauppa in the Stockman building in Helsinki. Whereas in England there are hardly a dozen decent book-shops outside the university towns, in Finland there is a book-shop in every large village, even within the Arctic Circle. And the equipment of the public libraries is something to make eyes used to the gloomy and impoverished institutions of most English country towns open wide in wonder. As for the Press, there were no less than 209 daily papers in circulation in 1936 (of which 23 were in the Swedish language) and 557 reviews. Circulation figures are not available, but 219,500,000 copies of registered journals and periodicals were distributed through the post alone in 1936; in other words, 59 copies for every man, woman and child of the population.

So much for quantity; the quality of the reading matter is naturally more difficult to assess. The book-shops sell an unusually high proportion of books in foreign languages. In the libraries books on theology and philosophy, history and travel are in greater demand than novels. The newspapers cannot rely on advertisements to keep down their costs, for newspaper advertising is relatively unprofitable in a small country; nor can they rely on sensationalism and the appeal of the special edition to keep up their circulation, for the simple reason that most of their readers are regular subscribers who change their paper only when they change their political views or—which often comes to the same thing —their job. Reading has not yet become the opium of the people. Again we appear to be approaching the conclusion that the Finns are also among the most cultured of peoples.

It may well be objected that culture is not to be measured by literacy and the prevalence of the reading habit. Book-learning in Europe seems to vary inversely with the temperature, the colder the climate the more books read. The Scots, the Scandinavians and the Finns read more than the Spaniards, the French and the Italians, yet who will say that the northerners are more highly cultured? In Spain, as Madariaga wrote with pardonable hyperbole, "illiterates speak like Seneca, sing like Blake and behave like Louis XIV." It may be urged with a certain amount of truth that the Finns have made book-learning a sort of fetish. They have concentrated on acquiring information rather than on understanding it, on learning rather than on knowledge. This is of course an invariable concomitant of education in a new country—it is the pet weakness of the U.S.A. and of the U.S.S.R.—but its appearance in Finland is not to be accounted for by the newness of the country. Centuries before the great plains of North America were colonized, centuries before the Russian serfs were emancipated, the Finns were a comparatively literate people. In the seventeenth century Bishop Gezelius insisted that Finns of all ages should take reading lessons from the pastor; in the eighteenth the Lutheran Church decreed that no one might be confirmed who could not read, and no one might be married who had not been confirmed. The Finns' faith in the written word has its roots far back in their pre-Christian culture. According to Shamanistic beliefs, words had a magic power. In the Kalevala the man who knew the sacred word and its origin was a magician. This power became transferred to the printed word, which was believed to have a permanence which nothing could alter. Hence the literal-mindedness of the contemporary Finn; "It must be true, I saw it in a book," is a remark more often heard in the Finnish than in the British working-classes. Hence too the legal-mindedness of the Finn, his love of forensic argument and litigation, and his insistence upon living under a written constitution.

This legal-mindedness goes far to account for the remarkable political stability of Finland. At the same time it has been responsible for giving the Finns an international reputation as legal quibblers. To give one rather trivial example: on the eve of the Los Angeles Olympic

Games of 1932 the runner Paavo Nurmi was disqualified as a professional. There is no doubt that in the general sense of the word Nurmi was a professional; there is also no doubt that according to the strict interpretation of the written rules governing professionalism Nurmi was not a professional. Finnish public opinion held to the letter of the law and was—and still is—outraged by the disqualification.

Veneration for the power of the written word has been responsible for the rapid development of education in Finland. But the most cursory study of the educational system will show that there is less emphasis on purely academic studies and more on vocational and physical training in the Finnish than in, for example, the English system. In England children are compelled to attend an elementary school between their fifth and their fourteenth birthday. It is generally recognized that the instructional value of schooling in the first of these years is nil; there is no point of beginning to teach a child the three R's at the age of five. It is also generally recognized that the value of an additional year at school would be enormous, but so far all attempts to raise the compulsory school age to fifteen have failed; the price, it has been held, is too high. In Finland all children attend elementary schools between the age of seven and thirteen, and go on until their fifteenth birthday to advanced schools where they follow a vocational course to prepare them for their life's work. The difficulties of transport in such a sparsely populated country might well have been accepted as an insuperable obstacle to universal education, but the authorities have overcome them by providing free transport or board-and-lodging allowances for all children who live more than five kilometres from a school. In England only twenty children out of every hundred go to secondary schools. There they follow an almost exclusively academic course, all taking the School Certificate examination which is based on the standards required for entrance to the universities; they are concentrating, in so far as they concentrate at all, on training themselves for clerical jobs as "white-collar workers." In Finland 40 per cent of the children go on to secondary schools. These are of two types, Classical schools where Latin and Greek are taught, and Modern where the emphasis is on mathematics and modern languages. In each for the first five years the pupils follow a course designed to prepare them for specific careers; after this there is a senior course of two or three years in preparation for the civil service, the teachers' training colleges, or the university. Towards the cost of secondary education the State paid 1,467 marks and the local authorities 944 marks for every pupil in 1936. For the pupils secondary education is free (except for nominal fees of a couple of pounds a year paid by the well-to-do).

As far as universities are concerned it may well be that England has little to learn from Finland. Hardly any Finnish scholars, with the exception of Professor Westermarck, the sociologist, and Dr. Tancred Borenius, the connoisseur, are known outside specialist circles in this country. Hardly any prominent English scholars, with the exception of Professor John Dover Wilson, have worked at Helsinki. But there are three points worth noting about the Finnish university system. First, all tuition at Helsinki University is free of charge, the expense being borne by the State which contributes some 33,000,000 marks a year to the university chest. Secondly the proportion of undergraduates to the whole population is remarkably high: one in every five hundred is in attendance at one of the three universities.[1] (In the United Kingdom the proportion is roughly one in 885.) Thirdly, in answer to the charge of bookishness levelled at Finnish education, Helsinki was the first university to establish faculties of Domestic Science and Physical Culture.

It is indeed precisely in the least bookish of educational institutions that most striking progress has been made: in the technical, agricultural and commercial colleges. The Trade Schools, of which examples are to be found in every town, have reached a surprising level of equipment and efficiency. "The most wonderful school I have ever seen," wrote a correspondent in the leading article of *The Times Educational Supplement* of 1 May, 1937, "is a trade school at Viipuri. Here I saw boys turning out every conceivable kind of woodwork and metal-work of excellent design and workmanship. Orders for painting motor cars, for dressmaking, furniture and other work are taken from the townspeople, and the proceeds contribute about 60 per cent of the total cost of the school's upkeep. There are many kinds of trade school—technical, industrial, commercial, agricultural— giving instruction in all branches of industry, in forestry, dairy-farming, or horticulture, and special establishments where girls learn advanced housewifery, homecrafts or weaving." In complete contrast to these purely instructional centres are the Folk Schools of which there are at present only eleven in Finland. They are modelled on the principles of the Danish pioneers Grundtvig and Kold. Young men and women, usually between eighteen and twenty years of age, live for a season under the same roof as their tutors

[1] In 1936 Helsinki University had 6,631 students and 315 teachers; Abo Akademi, the Swedish-speaking college at Turku, had 310 students and 49 teachers; and the Finnish-speaking University at Turku had 305 students and 39 teachers.

who aim at arousing intellectual curiosity rather than at imparting information, familiarizing their pupils with the cultural background of their country, with the historical development of the social and practical arts and sciences.

In short, if culture is to be measured by education, Finland must take a high place among the nations of the world. And if education is to be measured by the amount allotted to it by the Government, Finland must rank as the highest, for the State devotes nearly one-seventh of its annual expenditure to education.

The most obvious way of measuring a culture is by its arts and crafts. As far as the latter are concerned it must be admitted that the price of westernization—in the standard of living and the social services, in education and the status of women—has been the loss of many of the old skills of pre-industrial days. The skills of agriculture and husbandry are of course still practised, more thoroughly perhaps in Finland than in most other civilized countries, but a thousand domestic crafts are being forgotten. Except on the more isolated farms the country women no longer spin and weave their flax and wool, no longer make the clothes for the family; all the men and most of the women wear cheap factory-made garments in the standard Western style. The girls still weave the "ryijy," the knotted-pile rugs and covers for their bridal beds, but they copy the traditional designs—the *Tree of Life*, *Winter*, the *Coming of Spring* and the rest—slavishly from printed patterns. Men still throw the Vuoksi clay and glaze pots for their own use, but lead-glazed earthenware is forbidden for cooking purposes under the Poisons Act of 1888. They still make baskets of reeds or birch-bark and wooden casks to hold their ale, but they no longer fashion spoons and tubs from juniper, no longer make the heavy carved wooden presses for the family clothes-chest. Wooden chests and utensils, ryijy rugs and dyed linens are still made—to be sold to tourists. The ancient skills have degenerated into arts-and-crafts. Even the reindeer boots and *puukka* (knives) that were once the pride of Finland have been degraded to the tourist market. At Mariehamn in the Åland Islands Captain Gustav Ericson maintains a fleet of three-masted schooners. They ply for cargoes, bringing the early grain from Australia to England every year, but they pay their way only because Captain Ericson runs them uninsured. Twelve out of the sixteen large square-rigged sailing ships on Lloyd's Register are Captain Ericson's. These, the last of the tall ships, are a splendid survival. They can never be anything more. The motor boat has transformed the boat-building craft, and the skills which Finns developed through long centuries of sail have been frustrated by the iron and steam ship.

One is tempted to deplore this passing of the ancient crafts, especially after a visit to Estonia where so many of them are still practised with the old patient care. Finland has bought her progress with a great price, but even to the craftsman's eye it must be recognized as progress. The Finns have already gone some way towards transmuting their handicrafts into industrial crafts—no one who visited the Paris Exposition of 1937 could doubt that; but they have still a long way to go. Good work in glass is turned out by the Riihimaki and Karhula factories; in both the best available artists are employed as designers, but they have never recovered from the loss of Henry Ericcson, and it is a bad sign that Finns are so complacent about their products. Some good mass-produced pottery comes from the great kilns of the Arabia factory, but on the whole quality has been sacrificed to cheapness, except in the case of "purely artistic articles" which are made in a separate department which has not yet justified its existence. Wooden furniture, which Finns should be specially qualified to make well, is going through an experimental period. The heavy nineteenth-century styles which were copied from Germany and Sweden—all inlay and moulding and upholstery—have been succeeded by their antithesis—sketchy objects more suitable to a cosmopolitan café than to the domestic atmosphere of Finland, tables that are a gesture rather than a convenience, chairs that are neither durable nor comfortable. No doubt it is unfair to pass judgment during this experimental phase. Some excellent work is being done, particularly in manufacturing birch-wood furniture by factory processes, and modern Finnish furniture is extraordinarily successful when it has been designed specifically by the architect of a building, as in the case of some of Alvar Aalto's work.

Architecture indeed is the most flourishing of Finnish arts. The inspiration of Sweden is still strong, but Finland has produced in this century half a dozen men of international reputation whose different styles are all in a real sense national. There are no finer railway stations than Saarinen's buildings at Viipuri and (especially) at Helsinki; Sonck must rank among the first of modern church-architects; and Siren's Parliament House, with its formal pillared façade, is the first place of pilgrimage for tourists to Finland. The work of these three men has been chiefly in local granite, but other mediums have not been neglected. Red brick has been used to excellent effect for the tenement houses of the new Toolo quarter of the capital, and concrete goes as well with the clear light and bright colours of

Finland as it does with the very different atmosphere of New York. In this latter medium the work of Aalto is outstanding. Though still a young man, he has half a dozen satisfactory buildings in Turku to his credit and a dozen in other parts of the country. His *chef d'œuvre* is the public library at Viipuri, a low flat-roofed structure set among the trees in the central garden square of the city. Here he has made the best of roof lighting and roof heating, of light birch desks and chairs, and of unobtrusive devices for the muffling of sound. It is a revelation to find that a library can be airy and spacious, comfortable and attractive without forfeiting its air of studious and secluded calm.

In some buildings the new materials have been used in a way that shocks the purists. The Church of Mikael Agricola in Helsinki, for example: there is nothing to complain of in the red-brick exterior surmounted by its copper *flèche*, but the narrow arches of the nave are in concrete and it is objected that it is no function of concrete to imitate the Gothic. On the whole, however, functionalism without formalism is the characteristic of the new work. The old cult of massiveness for its own sake is giving way to a lighter touch. The special *forte* of modern Finnish architecture is the close relation between structure and external decoration; almost every new public building shows an harmonious understanding between architect, builder, sculptor and decorator.

Music, too, is a flourishing art now that Finns have grown out of the cantele. For generations musical development was held up, as Acerbi noted in 1799, "on account of the imperfection of their national instrument, and the attachment and veneration with which they have preserved it. . . . The whole compass of their music consists of five notes and with these five notes they play, they dance, and recite

225

their poetry and verses. . . . It is easy to imagine the melancholy and monotonous effect of their music, as well as the impossibility of improving it, until they shall abandon their five-stringed instrument."

The union between nationalism and music proved strangely fruitful, producing good instrumental work as well as memorable patriotic songs. Nearly all Finnish music from the middle of the nineteenth century to the first quarter of the twentieth was founded on folk tunes and on themes from the *Kalevala*; Pacius's operas, Sibelius's early symphonic poems (of which *Kullervo* created an unparalleled sensation when first performed in 1892), Melartin's six symphonies and Madetoja's symphonies and operas fall into this category. But the danger that Finnish music would be bound for ever to folk lore and folk themes has been overcome, and the younger composers—among whom Kilpinen and Klami should be noted—are working independently of them. The pre-eminence of Sibelius might also have become a danger, but he has proved not so much a model for imitators as an inspiration for independent composers. The Conservatory, which was founded in 1882, has fulfilled its function by educating rather than instructing musicians, by developing rather than conserving music. Finns are justified in regretting that Sibelius is the only one of their composers and Aino Ackté and Aulikki Rautawaara the only singers to be popular abroad, if their popularity has given the impression that other Finnish musicians are second-rate. The Helsinki Opera is one of the best north of Berlin and, to descend the scale, the orchestra that plays at Kapelli under the baton of Sibelius's son-in-law must be one of the best café orchestras in Europe.

In paint the Finns have been less happy. It is a more

sophisticated medium than architecture or music, and therefore not to be looked for in a high state of development among a peasant people. Finland produced no painters of note until the latter part of the nineteenth century, when there arose in Edelfelt and Gallen-Kallela two men who were justly admired by a generation whose god was Millais. Impressionism was brought to Finland by Magnus Enckell, but nobody should go north to study impressionism. Many contemporaries—Sallinen and Collin, for example—are doing good work and it is surprising to find official portraiture reaching such a high standard (as for instance in Wilho Sjöstrom's portrait of Mannerheim in Vaasa Town Hall) but there is no livelihood to be earned by a painter in Finland; there are few private buyers and the State gives little or nothing of the encouragement to poster and decorative work that is given by the Soviet Government. Public authorities are more generous in their patronage of sculptors, as is shown by the deserved prominence of the work of young Väinö Aaltonen.

Architecture, music and painting are international arts; Finland's achievement in them can be appreciated by those who have eyes to see and ears to hear, without any knowledge of the people or of either of their languages. But with literature it is different. The literature of a small country must depend, for general appreciation, upon translation, and it is Finland's misfortune that her peculiar literary quality defies translation. Finland's writers, alike in poetry and in prose, in Swedish and in Finnish, are predominantly lyrical. How can a lyric be translated? Add to this the facts that her writers are preoccupied to an unusual degree with landscape and the spirit-of-place and that they have held themselves aloof from foreign influences (not following the

Swedish men of letters, for example, in their exodus to Paris), and it can be realized that Finnish literature must remain a closed book to the outside world. The Swedish poets of Finland, from Runeberg to Bertel Gripenberg, are well enough known in Scandinavia, but the modern poets in Finnish, from the individualist Leino to the academic Koskenniemi, are not known even there. The novelists have fared a little better. Aleksis Kivi is almost worthy of a place on the bookshelf beside Cervantes and Rabelais; Juhani Aho might be appreciated by lovers of Maupassant, Arvid Järnefelt by followers of Tolstoi, and Linnankoski may be recommended to readers who like Selma Lagerlöf. The most typically Finnish of the contemporary novelists is Sillanpää; it is a misfortune that more of his books have not been translated into English.[1] But with novelists as with poets the lyrical tendency militates against their appreciation outside Finland.

The same limitation applies, though to a lesser degree, to the drama. The Finnish genius has found less expression in the theatre than in any other art. Kivi wrote one great play, *The Village Cobblers*, but Finland has produced no Tchehov, no Ibsen, no Strindberg, though one or two of the contemporaries are shaping well, particularly Helea Wuolijoki, whose play *The Women of Niskavuori* has been translated into most European languages.[2] Yet the theatre is extremely popular in Finland. There are twenty per-

[1] There is only one good translator from Finnish into English: Alex Matson. (A list of some translations into English is given in the Bibliography.)

[2] It was produced in London at the Queen's Theatre in 1937 under the title of *Women of Property*, and was very well received by the critics, though not by the public, whose support did not justify a run of more than a fortnight—a not unusual fate for a serious play in Shaftesbury Avenue in July.

manent Finnish theatres and three Swedish, and the number of private semi-amateur play-producing societies run by workers' clubs and other societies amounts to nearly 4,000 —an extraordinary number for a population of under four millions. The Finns take their theatre in deadly earnest; Monsieur Perret has found a village in the far north with no more than a thousand inhabitants where the workers' club put on Ibsen, Strindberg, Molière and Tolstoi in the course of a single season and made a financial success of it. On the whole the theatre in Finland is a medium of education and of propaganda rather than of amusement, the propaganda being not that of class against class but of language against language, for the Swedish-speaking community will strain every nerve and spend every penny rather than be outdone by the Finnish-speaking actors. Here at least the language controversy has turned to good account.

In summing up we are thrown back on a conclusion which there is little uncontroversial evidence to support: it is that the arts of Finland, having grown out of the folk stage and having lost the initial impetus of the nationalist movement, are struggling through a period of transition from which, except in the fields of architecture and music, there are few signs of rapid emergence.

The difficult nature of this transition-period in the inner life of the Finns is reflected in their religion. By nature they are a religious people, in the sense of being conscious of affinity with the supernatural. From the time of the Reformation to the nineteenth century the Lutheran Church seems to have provided a satisfactory vehicle for their devotions. At the beginning of the nineteenth century there was a great Pietist revival, but revivalism soon exhausts itself and towards the end of the century consciousness of affinity with nature—with the Finnish land and folk—became stronger than any sense of supernatural affinity. Now that the aims of nationalism are to some extent achieved, one might expect to see signs of a return to religion. But there are none. Good works abound, but not faith. The Salvation Army prospers because of the social succour it affords, and the Young Men's and Young Women's Christian Associations for the same reason. Theosophy and the occult sciences have many adherents, but as a means of escape rather than as an integral religion. The Lutheran Church is still strong, but as a social institution, an Establishment. The Roman and the Orthodox Churches keep up their tiny numbers, but they are not growing. For the masses the conscious focus of religious feeling is still nationalism.

Nationalism—the sense of common traditions and a common destiny—has saved Finnish culture from extinction. The Finns have used the material forces of civilization as the guardian and educator of that culture. So far these forces have not become their master, yet a certain amount of materialism has been the price of Finland's progress. It is not for us who knew no famines in the nineteenth century to condemn the concentration of the Finns on improving their natural conditions; but we may well be permitted to wonder where the progress that has ended those famines is going to lead. Wherever it may be the general direction will not be far from that of the nations of the Western world, for Finland is the eastern outpost of Western civilization.

BIBLIOGRAPHY

Only works in English are listed here. For a bibliography of recently published books in German, French, Italian, Spanish and Dutch, see the Finland Year Book; *for works in Swedish, see the article "Finland" in the* Svensk Uppslagsbok.

REFERENCE

There are three useful books of general reference, all published in Helsinki and obtainable from the Akateeminen Kirjakauppa:—

The Finland Year Book.

The Atlas of Finland.

Finland: The Country, Its People and Institutions (1926).

TRAVEL

The best general discursive books are still:—

J. ACERBI—*Travels Through Sweden, Finland and Lapland* (1802).

ROSALIND TRAVERS—*Letters from Finland* (1911).

T. W. ATCHLEY—*Finland* (1931).

Others in chronological order are:—

E. D. CLARKE—*Travels in Europe, Asia and Africa*, Vol. X (1824).

M. C. CLIVE-BAYLEY—*Vignettes from Finland* (1895).

A. TWEEDIE—*Through Finland in Carts* (1897).

H. DE WINDT—*Finland as it is* (1901).

G. RENWICK—*Finland To-day* (1911).

E. YOUNG—*Finland: The Land of a Thousand Lakes* (1912).

A. READE—*Finland and the Finns* (1915).

R. MEDILL—*Finland and its People* (1925).

A. MacCALLUM SCOTT—*Suomi: The Land of the Finns* (1926).

FRANK FOX—*Finland To-day* (1926).

KAY GILMOUR—*Finland* (1931).

A. J. PEARSON—*The Land of a Thousand Lakes* (1932).

AGNES ROTHERY—*Finland* (1936).

HALLIDAY SUTHERLAND—*Lapland Journey* (1938).

HISTORY

For the origins see:—

J. C. BROWN—*The People of Finland in Archaic Times* (1892).

J. ABERCROMBY—*The Pre- and Proto-Historic Finns* (1898).

For the mediaeval and earlier modern period:—

J. STEFANSON—*Sweden and Denmark, with Finland and Iceland* (1924).

R. NISBET BAIN—*Scandinavia* (1905).

For the nineteenth century:—

L. MECHELIN (Editor)—*Finland in the Nineteenth Century.*

J. R. DANIELSON-KALMARI—*Finland's Union with the Russian Empire* (1891).

J. R. FISHER—*Finland and the Tsars* (1899).

For the twentieth century:—

J. BUCHAN (Editor)—*The Baltic and the Caucasian States* (1920).

W. M. GRAHAM—*New Governments of Eastern Europe* (1928).

R. L. BUELL (Editor)—*New Governments in Europe* (1934).

ECONOMICS

JÄRVINEN and others—*Trade and Industry of Finland* (1922).

L. HARMAJA—*Effects of the War in Finland* (1933).

KEITH JOPSON—*Economic Conditions in Finland* (Department of Overseas Trade, 1936).

The Times Trade and Engineering Supplement (June 1936).

Finnish Trade Review (Helsinki).

Bank of Finland Monthly Bulletin (Helsinki).

SPECIAL SUBJECTS

E. VAN CLEEF—*The Republic Farthest North: The Response of Finnish Life to its Geographical Environment* (Ohio, 1929).

J. H. WUORINEN—*The Prohibition Experiment in Finland* (N.Y., 1931).

Nationalism in Modern Finland (N.Y., 1931).

A. LEHTONEN—*The Church of Finland* (Helsinki, 1927).

O. DONNER—*Brief Sketch of the Scottish Families in Finland and Sweden* (1884).

HENNING SÖDERHJELM—*The Red Insurrection in Finland* (1919).

C. C. M. MAYNARD—*Murmansk Venture* (1928).

THORSTEN ODHE—*Finland: A Nation of Co-operators* (1931).

LEO MECHELIN—*The Public Law of Finland* (1889).

M. W. GRAHAM—*Diplomatic Recognition of the Baltic States: Part I. Finland* (Berkeley, Calif., 1935).

W. MENTEITH (Editor)—*The Conquest of Finland 1808–1809* (1854).

L. INGMAN—*The Lapua Anti-Communist Movement* (Helsinki, 1930).

E. N. SETÄLÄ—*The Language Fight in Finland* (Helsinki, 1920).

KARL EKMAN—*Jean Sibelius* (Helsinki, 1935).

LILIAN STEVENSON—*Mathilde Wrede, Friend of Prisoners* (1925).

I. HALLSTEN—*The Position of Women in Finland* (Helsinki, 1925).

POEMS AND NOVELS

Of the .classics, *Kalevala* has been translated into English several times (the best version is W. F. Kirby's in Everyman's Library, 1907); translations of Runeberg's *Poems* and *Elk Hunters* were published by Kegan Paul in 1878 and 1879, and of his *Songs of Ensign Stahl* by Stechert & Co., of New York, in 1925. Kivi's immortal *Seven Brothers* was successfully translated by Alex Matson in 1929; Fisher Unwin published a translation of Juhani Aho's *Squire Hellman and Other Stories* in 1893, and Jarrolds a version of Zachris Topelius's romance, *The King's Ring*, in 1901.

Of contemporary authors the best books available in English are probably F. E. Sillanpää's *Fallen Asleep While Young* and *Meek Heritage.* Jarl Hemmer's *The Fool of Faith* and S. Salminen's *Katrina* give a good idea of modern Swedo-Finnish writing. J. Linnankoski's *Song of the Blood-Red Flower* is a best-seller in Finland, but the English translation is, to say the least, disappointing. Aino Kallas, a Finnish woman married to an Estonian, has written unforgettable stories about the land of her adoption in *Eros the Slayer* and *The White Ship.*

INDEX